# THE GRENADA REVOLUTION:

# WHY IT FAILED

# THE GRENADA REVOLUTION: WHY IT FAILED

ROBERT MILLETTE

MAHIN GOSINE

Studies In Pan-African Life

Amos N. Wilson, General Editor

Africana Research Publications New York

ISBN: 0-93324-00-5

# TABLE OF CONTENTS

To Stanford Lyman and Rocco Caporale:
Teachers, Mentors, Friends.

**MAHIN GOSINE** received his Ph.D. in Sociology from St. John's University. He has lectured at Nassau Community College, Hostos Community College, New York City Technical College, and John Jay College of Criminal Justice. Dr. Gosine is currently teaching in the Department of Social Sciences at Fordham University and the Department of Behavioral Sciences at New York Institute of Technology. He is the Author of Ethnic Heterogeneity and the Black Power Movement in Trinidad.

**ROBERT MILLETTE** graduated with his Ph.D. in Sociology from the New School for Social Research. He has taught at William Patterson College, LaGuardia Community College, and Talladega College. He is currently Chairman of the Department of Sociology and Human Services at Lincoln University. Dr. Millette is the author of New Grenada in Brooklyn: Social Stratification and Adaptation Among First Generation Immigrants.

# LIST OF ABBREVIATIONS

A.D.C.C.P. – American Department of the Cuban Communist Party
A.F.S.U. - Armed Forces of the Soviet Union
A.S.N.E. - American Society of Newpaper Editors
A.T.W.U. - Allied and Technical Workers Union
C.A.R.D. - Campaign Against Racial Discrimination
C.A.R.I.C.O.M. - Caribbean Common Market
C.B.S. - Columbia Broadcasting System
C.I.A. - Central Intelligence Agency
C.I.W.U. - Commerical and Industrial Workers Union
D.O.D. - Department of Defense
E.C.C.B. - Eastern Caribbean Central Bank
E.C.D. - Eastern Caribbean Dollars
E.E.C. - European Economic Community
E.P.S.A. - Essential Public Services Act
F.A. - Firearms Act
F.B.I. - Federal Bureau of Investigation
G.A.U. - Grenada Agriculturalist Union
G.C.C. - Grenada Chamber of Commerce
G.C.E. - General Certificate of Education
G.D.M. - Grenada Democratic Movement
G.D.P. - Gross Domestic Product
G.M.F.D. - Grenada Movement for Freedom and Democracy
G.M.M.W.U. - Grenada Manual and Mental Workers Union
G.N.P. - Grenada National Party
G.N.P. - Gross National Product
G.P.S. - Grenada Police Service
GRENLEC - Grenada Electricity Company
G.T.U. - Grenada Teachers Union
G.T.U.C. - Grenada Trade Union Council
G.U.L.P. - Grenada United Labor Party
G.U.T. - Grenada Union of Teachers
G.W.U. - Grenada Workers Union
I.A.C.H.R. - Inter/American Commission on Human Rights
I.M.F. - International Monetary Fund
J.E.W.E.L. - Joint Endeavour for Welfare, Education and Liberation
K.G.B. - Committee of State Security
L.A.C. - Legal Aid Clinic
M.A.P. - Movement for Assemblies of the People
M.B.P.M. - Maurice Bishop Patriotic Movement

## LIST OF ABBREVIATIONS CONT'D.

N.A. - Newspaper Act
N.A.T.O. - North Atlantic Treaty Organization
N.D.P. - National Democratic Party
N.J.M. - New Jewel Movement
N.N.P. - New National Party
N.W.O. - National Women's Organization
N.Y.O. - National Youth Organization
O.A.S. - Organization of American States
O.A.S.E.U. - Organization of American States Emergency Unit
O.E.A.R. - Organization for Educational Advancement and Research
O.E.C.S. - Organization of Eastern Caribbean States
P.A.A. - Port Authority Act
P.O.A. - Public Order Act
P.R.A. - People's Revolutionary Army
P.R.A.F. - People's Revolutionary Armed Forces
P.R.G. - People's Revolutionary Government
P.R.M. - People's Revolutionary Militia
P.S.C. - Public Service Commission
P.W.U. - Public Workers Union
R.F.G. - Radio Free Grenada
R.G.P.F. - Royal Grenada Police Force
R.M.C. - Revolutionary Military Council
S.J.L.P. - St. John's Labor Party
S.W.W.U. - Seamen and Waterfront Workers Union
T.A.W.U. - Technical and Allied Workers Union
T. & T. - Trinidad and Tobago
T.Y.W.C. - Trevoli Young Workers Cooperative
U.F.O. - Unidentified Flying Object
U.N. - United Nations
U.S. - United States
U.S.P.C. - United States Peace Corps
U.S.S.R. - Union of Soviet Socialist Republic
W.B. - World Bank
W.B.R. - World Bank Report
W.I.S.S. - West Indian Students Society
W.P.A. - War Powers Act
W.P.R. - War Powers Resolution

# PREFACE

The intent of this study is to ascertain the reasons why the Grenada revolution failed. In order to accomplish this task, we examined and analyzed several questions. Among the most important questions we asked were: (1) Did the revolution fail to succeed because the leaders did not fully understand the true meaning of revolution? (2) Did the movement fail because the leadership did not fully understand the historical situation and socio-economic aspirations of the Grenadians? (3) Did it fail because of internal conflicts between and among the leaders of the revolution? (4) Or did the revolution fail because of outside interferences? In attempting to come to grips with these questions, we discovered that the revolution had two sides, a public and a private. The public side told the Grenadians that the revolution was achieving its goals and objectives. The private side or the reality of the revolution, meanwhile, told another story. It was common knowledge to members of the Central Committee that the revolution lacked 'ideological purity ', a central focus; and, therefore, was not accomplishing its intended mission. Needless to say this side of the revolution was closely guarded from public view.

But there were also other reasons why the revolution encountered difficulty. Among them were the inability of the leadership to grapple with the historical condition of the working class; the embarking upon an ideology that was contrary to the aspirations and expectations of the masses of the working class Grenadians; the paucity of capital and resources that were vital to the success of the revolution; the actions and ideas of the leadership that tended to alienate large sections of the national population; the materializing of an intense internal power struggle between and among the core leaders, and the military weakness of the revolution to successfully defend itself against the armed might of the United States.

Working on this study was a difficult task and had it not been for the help we received from certain individuals, both in Grenada and in the United States, the study might not have been completed. Therefore, there are many people to whom we would like to express our gratitude. Our first acknowledgement goes to the many Grenadians who, at risk of being labeled destabilizers, supplied us with data during the rule of the revolutionary government and after the American intervention. These individuals clearly understood that the "full weight of the revolution" would have been leveled against them, if they were caught sending us information. From these individuals, we learned that there was a public as well as private side to the revolution. In order to protect the anonymity of these individuals, we will not name any of them.

In the United States, a number of people were equally helpful. Deserving special mention are Augustine and Mary Hopkins and their children Kenneth and Charmaine who, more than anyone else, painstakingly assisted with the collection of data. To them, we wish to extend a warm and heartfelt "Thank you". We are also eternally grateful to Professor Thomas McDonald of Fordham University; Professor Leslie Ault and Dr. Mary Koutsoudaki of Hostos Community College, the City University of New York; Dr. Alice Richardson of New York City Technical College; Dr. Michael Wubnig and Dr. Robert Goldblatt of New York Institute of Technology; Professor Bertram Gregg, Mr. Everlee Jones and Mrs Juliet Smith of Talledega College; Dr. Joseph N. Gayles of Morehouse Medical School; Dr. Gloria Gayles of Spellman College; and Mr. and Mrs. Sydney Connell; Mrs. Bernadette Connell; and Mrs. Agnes Langdon who served as sounding boards for some of our ideas and provided the needed encouragement to complete the study. Our families, too, gave us the strength and necessary support as we spent long hours in the library or on the interview trail. We also wish to thank Professor Stanford Lyman of The New School for Social Research and Professor Rocco Caporale of St. John's University, our teachers and mentors, to both of whom this book is dedicated, for being instrumental in nurturing and moulding our careers as social scientists. To them, we are forever indebted. Finally, we wish to acknowledge that for all the shortcomings in this book, the responsibiity is ours.

R.E.M., New York City, October 19, 1984
M.G., New York City, October 19, 1984

# INTRODUCTION

# THE GRENADA REVOLUTION:

# WHY IT FAILED

On March 13, 1979, the government of Eric Matthew Gairy was overthrown by the People's Revolutionary Army (P.R.A.). The revolution propelled into political power a young English-trained lawyer named Maurice Bishop. The revolution, at the onset, had the overwhelming support of Grenadians both at home and abroad. A poll conducted by the authors found that 98% of Grenadians who reside in New York supported the People's Revolutionary Government (P.R.G.) The P.R.G. also had strong support from many Caribbean Governments.

The P.R.G. lost most of its popular support when Bishop reneged on his promise to hold open and free elections. Approximately three months after the so called "populist revolution", Bishop and the P.R.G. significantly increased the size of the P.R.A., imprisoned its opposition, formed close ties with Cuba, and systematically harassed the management of the local newpaper. The P.R.G., in spite of growing criticisms, was seen by many Grenadians as being unified and having a sense of purpose. Bishop's alleged charismatic leadership was mainly responsible for this appearance of unity. Data collected after the American invasion clearly documents the differences in ideology and direction that existed among ranking members of the P.R.G.

At a meeting of the Central Committee on September 25, 1983, Bishop was criticized for weak leadership. The minutes of that meeting further state: "Maurice Bishop has tremendous strengths that are necessary for the process, but these by themselves cannot carry the party out of its present crisis. The qualities that are also needed are those of: (1) a Leninist level of organization and discipline, (2) great depth in ideological clarity and tactics clarity, (3) brilliance in strategy at tactics and (4) the capacity to exercise Leninist supervision, control and guidance of all areas of party work are today not present in the comrade."[1] The report continued to

1

point out that the Central Committee has been making errors for at least 12 months. "The unwillingless of its members to study, think, take hard decisions, and struggle for its implementation have led Cde. Bernard Coard to resign from the Central Committee September 1982".,It was decided at that meeting that Maurice Bishop be asked to share power with his deputy, Bernard Coard. After considering the recommendation of the Central Committee, he refused the idea of "joint leadership" Bishop's unwillingless to share power with Coard, a hard line Marxist, apparently led to the Prime Minister's death.

On October 13, 1983, Bishop was placed under house arrest. On October 19, thousands of his supporters freed him and led him through the streets of St. George's to Fort Rupert. At the Fort they were confronted by the P.R.A. who fired on the crowd. Bishop, three of his cabinet ministers, and two labor leaders were killed. On Thursday, October 20, many Caribbean countries and institutions condemned the "military coup" in Grenada. On October 25, Grenada was invaded by U.S. Marines, Army Rangers, and troops from six Caribbean nations.

Like the March 13, 1979 Revolution, the American intervention was welcomed by many Grenadians at home and abroad. An editorial in *The Grenadian Voice* says "we commend President Reagan and all the Caribbean leaders for recognizing the need for intervention in Grenada and having the courage of their conviction knowing the calamity that would be heaped on their heads," seems to capture the feelings of many Grenadians.

The aim of this work is not simply to trace the demise of the Grenada Revolution. Several questions will have to be asked and answered if we are to get at the facts. For instance, what events led to the revolution? Did the New Jewel Movement's (N.J.M.) philosophy alienate the middle and upper classes? What was the impact of Marxist/Leninist views of the N.J.M. on the Grenada populace? The N.J.M. was organized by Maurice Bishop and Unison Whiteman to oppose the dictatorial rule of Eric Gairy. This movement was determined to take political power from Gairy and give it to the masses.

This study is not designed to develop "scientific laws." We, like Dilthey, Sombart, Rickert and Weber, are concerned with "interpretative meanings". Unlike the positivist, we intend to look at the world through the actors' eyes and make sense of it through the means they employ.₂ With this objective in mind, it would be helpful to see how Grenadians viewed the N.J.M.

The N.J.M. from the beginning of the 1970's captured the imagination of the youth and the unemployed. The N.J.M. held public meetings, daily private meetings, conducted what they called "People's Trials", advocated better housing conditions, more employment, better health facilities, and the development of a new economic order. In addition, they published a newspaper called the "Jewel".

The N.J.M.'s organizational skills, propaganda machinery, and their ability to attract mass support were quite impressive. For example, on November 4, 1973, the N.J.M. held a meeting in Sea Moon in the parish of St. Andrew's. That meeting was called a "People's Congress". A resolution entitled "The People's Indictment" was passed.₃

Esley Carberry, secretary of the N.J.M., wrote the then Prime Minister Sir Eric Gairy, Governmental Ministers, and Senators calling upon them to resign effective November 18, 1973. The People's Indictment accused the Prime Minister of openly condoning the shooting of "ten peaceful and unarmed demonstrators", ruling the people by fear, hiring known criminals, squandering the people's money, and neglecting the basic needs of the citizenry.

As the opposition  party , the N.J.M. did not say what it would do to improve the basic needs of Grenadians in such areas as housing, medical facilities, education, transportation, clothing, and food. After the revolution, Grenadians looked to the P.R.G. to provide the things it promised at the People's Congress. However the P.R.G. did not have the financial resources to actualize its promises.

We will attempt to show that the P.R.G. was unable to move from a popular opposition party to an effective government of the country because, once in power, it was plagued with a host of problems. These problems were lack of a common political ideology within the leadership of the N.J.M., and lack of a common economic policy, lack of experience within the ranks of the leadership, foreign domination, lack of support from the landed aristocracy and the middle classes.In short, the transition from opposition to government was never truly made.

For all practical purposes the revolution turned sour approximately four  months after the March 13, 1979, uprising. Bishop, the populist, and his deputy, Bernard Coard, had two different agendas. Bishop wanted a populist movement while Coard advocated a hard line Marxist/Leninist state. This line of thought will be further developed in a later chapter. It is sufficient to point out, at this time, that Bishop allegedly wanted to build. a "Democratic" state. This infuriated Coard and his followers who accused the Prime Minister of not having ideological clarity.

This so-called lack of ideological clarity and firmness led several Grenadians to question the direction of the revolution. Four months after the revolution D. Sinclair Dabero wrote in his book entitled *The Grenada Revolution,* "Yes, Grenada today is a land of hope, for the vast majority of its people. But this hope is based not upon performance, but upon promise ...",₂ Many Grenadians saw the leaders of the P.R.G. as young and untried men who rose to power because of their promises. The leaders were accused of establishing close ties with Cuba, of massive arms build-up, of creating a one-party state, and of imprisoning several loyal members of the party. Grenadians were afraid that they might lose many of their basic freedoms which, according to one former Jewel supporter, they had under Gairy.

The Grenada revolution gives social thinkers an opportunity to raise the following questions: (1) Is the Marxist/Leninist form of government the answer to the Caribbean? (2) Can small, poor, undeveloped countries like Grenada be truly non-aligned? (3) Can a revolution solve the economical, political, and social needs of the people? What must so-called revolutionaries know about the culture of the people in order for their governments to succeed?

The overthrow of Gairy was welcomed because it signaled the beginning of a new day. In Machiavelli's book, *The Prince,* he said that it is easy to persuade people to seize power, but difficult to keep them in that persuasion.₄ Months after the rebellion Bishop was accused of taking Grenada into the Cuban, and therefore, Russian Camp. To counteract this accusation the Prime Minister reiterated time and time again that Grenada was in nobody's backyard. Dabreo said that "if Bishop is able to convince those doubting Grenadians about his sincerity on this subject, then he would have achieved a major political victory".₃ Bishop and his colleagues were accused of misleading the Grenadian people. Grenadians pointed to the fact that the Revolutionary Government advocated and practiced socialist and communist teachings. The rhetoric of the P.R.G. included concepts which were anti-capitalist, and anti-imperialist. Many citizens as well as foreign observers, believed that the leadership of the N.J.M. was bent on spreading Communism throughout the Caribbean. The phrase that "Power comes from the barrel of a gun" was often carried as a slogan of the N.J.M.'s paper. The critics of the N.J.M. accused it of making heroes of Communist personalties living or dead, and of developing the economy of Grenada along lines that would even-

4

tually lead to state ownership. In addition, most N.J.M. leaders, including Bishop, Whiteman, and Coard, were Marxists.[3]

People worried because of the speed with which these Communistic changes were carried out. A respondent, and former member of the N.J.M., told the authors that "Bishop and the rest of these nasty guys fooled all Grenadians. We wanted change but not the kind of foolishness that Maurice is practicing. I hate to admit it, but we were much better off under Gairy even though he is a son-of-a-bitch. Only God knows when this oppression and suffering would end. I pray every night that Maurice will call an election. I am tired of seeing Grenada ruled by force and the Cubans." [5]

By July 1979, the honeymoon was over. "Unless the leaders become more aware of the undercurrent of fear, the fear of the greater loss of liberty, and of greater repression under the P.R.G. than was experienced under Gairy, they may well be heading for as great opposition from the people as they organized against Gairy."[3] Barry B. Levine says that the minutes of the September 25, 1983 meeting of the Central Committee of the N.J.M. "portrays a dismal picture of unimaginative leaders chained to an alien vocabulary".[7] He went on to say that the importation of this alien vocabulary led many Grenadians to distrust the motives of the P.R.G.

Bishop and the P.R.G. included much of Tanzania's Julius Nyerere's doctrine of "Christian Socialism" into their goals of teaching the peasantry self-sufficiency and self-pride. The Prime Minister in an interview with *The Black Scholar* said that his government would place emphasis on agriculture, fisheries, and tourism. He emphasized that this government intends to expand agro-industrialization using as a base the raw materials they produce. They would process cocoa, nutmeg and bananas.

The N.J.M. had a Utopian dream for solving many of Grenada's social, political and economic problems. The party's "Revolutionary Utopianism" did not work. The March 13, 1979, revolution did not bring about the results that Bishop and his men constantly spoke about. As promised, the people were not in control of their own destiny. "The party's Central Committee, not any people's assemblies, provided the leadership of what was called the P.R.G. Rather than a People's police force, the People's Revolutionary Armed Forces (P.R.A.F.), with former sergeant Hudson Austin now its commanding general, were trained and equipped by the Cubans. The East Germans trained the secret police."₇

The village assemblies were led by the inner circle of the N.J.M. Rather than grass roots agricultural developments, the P.R.G. spent most of its energies building the airport. Detention camps, loss of freedom of speech, and torture replaced elections. A new blueprint was revealing itself, a new description of the Grenadian reality. The major problem for the P.R.G. was that many Grenadians did not know or understand the new reality. It should also be pointed out that the leadership of the P.R.G. was split along ideological lines. The leaders did not agree on the definition of the situation. Not surprisingly, the regime split over the role the private sector was to play in economic development. Bishop felt that the state sector alone could not develop the economy. Needless to say, Coard disagreed. "The first sign that the typical succession battle in authoritarian socialist states was in full gear was Bernard Coard's call for a return to collective leadership."₇

Why did the Grenada revolution fail? In order to grapple with this question, we will examine the following: (1) Did the revolution fail because the leadership lied to Grenadians? (2) Did the revolution fail because of conflicting ideologies and dissentions within the P.R.G. and the N.J.M.? (3) Did the revolution fail to succeed because it lacked a religious base? (4) Did it fail because Bishop, unlike Eric Matthew Gairy, did not have the support of the masses? (5) Did the P.R.G.'s association with Cuba and other Communist countries alienate the middle and upper class followers? (6) Did the revolution fail because the P.R.G. and the N.J.M. spent too much time criticizing Gairy instead of rebuilding the country's economic and social structure?

**The Methods of the Study**

This study is not intended to criticize or praise the Grenada revolution. Instead, the main purpose is to get at real and not imagined meanings. According to Herbert Gans, "The essence of sociology,... is that it observes what people really do and say. It looks at the world from their perspective, unlike much literary writing, which often boils down to cataloguing their shortcomings from the author's perspective ...". To utilize Gans' method, the authors employed several research techniques. We used participant observation, intensive interviewing, questionnaires and telephone interviewing. Furthermore, data was gathered from books, journals, magazines, newspapers, letters, pamphlets, official records, and other sources. Since 1979, one of the authors of this book was involved in trying to restore democracy to Grenada. Therefore, we faced the danger of fitting our personal feelings into our conceptual categories. These hazards are present in any scientific endeavor, but they are mulitiplied when the researcher is personally involved in the group he or she is studying. This problem plagued the authors. We knew that the quality of our study hinged largely on our ability to comprehend human behavior which expresses meanings that we ordinarily would not entertain in our personal world. We understood that the only way in which our influence could be controlled is "through the development of methods for making subjective responses accessible to objective scrutiny during the several phases of the scientific process." [9] We tried to achieve this objective by maintaining the proper balance between detachment and involvement. We constantly reminded ourselves that our role should be that of social scientists and not that of political activists.

We agree with Stein when he says that team research is especially helpful in community studies because it broadens the dramatic range of the members. Having more than one person doing the study means that different avenues into the community can be established and various perspectives brought into focus that might escape the single investigation: "it creates a situation in which team members can control each other's tendencies toward over involvement or over detachment while the research is in progress and while the report is being written." [9] One of the authors, a Grenadian-American found it difficult, at times, to separate fact from fiction. His role of social scientist and political activist sometimes overlapped. The co-author, a Trinidadian-American and an expert on the Black Power movement, constantly reminded us of our role as social scientists. In seeking to get at multiple interpretations, many of the taken-for-granted about the Grenada revolution became topics for investigation. For example, we carefully examined concepts such as assemblies, people's law, people's work brigade, non-alignment, revolution, comrade, free Grenada, democracy, friends of Grenada, free election, legality. We quickly learned that these concepts meant one thing for the P.R.G. and something quite different for those who opposed the P.R.G. Therefore, it is important for us to understand that "the way we get at knowledge and the techniques we use to collect evidence are directly related to our image of reality and the way we think we know it.." [2] We carefully looked at the revolution through the actors' eyes. We listened, we observed, we asked questions, we attended rallies at which several interpretations of the revolution were discussed.

The collection of the data for this study started after the Grenada revolution. As a matter of fact, the authors wrote several articles outlining reasons why they thought the revolution would fail. We made our predictions based on data received from Grenadians at home and abroad. Participant observation, as a research tool, enabled us to detect that there were two responses to the revolution - the public and the private. The P.R.G. presented the public images while former supporters of the P.R.G., the N.J.M., and former members of the P.R.A. gave the private responses. The P.R.G. said publicly that the revolution was achieving its goals and objectives.

Our contacts with former supporters of government and ex-members of the militia told a different story. We were informed of internal conflicts within the ranks of the P.R.A. and N.J.M.. While visiting Grenada in 1979 we were informed by a member of the P.R.A. that the government was experiencing internal conflicts. He said: "the revolution will not last two years. Bishop and Coard are on two separate wave-lengths. Bishop wants a moderate form of socialism. Coard, on the other hand, is a hardcore Communist. Both he (Coard) and his wife Phyllis, are opposing Bishop."[10] We were also informed of personal confrontations between Phyllis and Angela, Bishop's wife. Anyone who mentioned these internal struggles were labeled destabilizers by the P.R.G. The major problem facing the authors was one of accurately assessing the definition of the situation.

Participant observation and intensive interviewing enabled us to listen to Grenadians as they constructed their reality. Many supported and continue to support Maurice. They saw him as a leader who could be trusted. Bishop was compared with Gairy, on one hand, and Coard on the other. His charismatic personality overshadowed his leadership abilities. A supporter of the P.R.G. told us that "Maurice is a good guy. We cannot return Grenada to Gairy's rule. Coard is a madman and he is definitely not the answer for Grenada. We do need to give Maurice a chance"[11]. Many Grenadians similarly defined the situation. They were afraid of Gairy's and Coard's leadership and therefore refused to examine and question the leadership of the P.R.G.. W.I. Thomas was correct when he said that if we define a situation as real, then it is real in its consequences. Many loyal supporters of the P.R.G. refused to believe that there were several political prisoners detained in Grenada without trial. Instead of questioning the closing of the local newspaper, the refusal to hold elections, the imprisonment of destabilizers, the torture and harassment of the P.R.G.'s opposition, the loyal supporters questioned the motives of anyone who raised concern about these events. With so much confusion and apprehension among supporters of the P.R.G., how can the participant observer make sense of the situation? Should we embrace the positivist approach and develop scientific knowledge of reality? We were not about to develop "scientific-laws" about the revolution. Instead, we were more concerned about understanding how the social actors interpreted the public and private images of the revolution.

Participant observation enabled the authors to penetrate the inner workings of the Grenadian community. The participant observer "must be able to see, to listen, and to feel sensitively the social interactions of which he becomes a part... He must question time and again whether he has perceived enough and whether his understandings are as accurate as he can make them"[12]. Our contacts with members of the P.R.A. and N.J.M. helped enable us to understand better the day-to-day operation of the revolution. These members provided us with the insider's view. We used this information as a guide for questioning that which was taken for granted. We were told that we simply do not understand the "progress and direction of the revolution." An engineer, and a friend of the authors, told us that we (the authors) are not revolutionaries and will not understand what is happening in Grenada. "The new government is trying to build a free and just society for all Grenadians. In order for this to be accomplished we have to place guys like you and ... under heavy manners. The colonial mentality will not permit people like yourself to see the light, the new beginning."[13] We agree with Jack D. Douglas when he says that "the background feelings and meanings are part of the members' ' natural attitude ' toward their world. To them these feelings and meanings are natural and normal, something anyone knows, at least anyone who is part of that world..."[14]

From 1979 to approximately 1983 the authors were called stupid, funny, dumb, and destabilizers whenever they questioned information normally taken for granted. We later found out that the public responses of the P.R.G. were defense mechanisms used to confuse the facts. Grenadians at home and abroad were afraid to criticize the P.R.G. Criticisms were dealt with swiftly and harshly. Several Grenadians who criticized the revolution were "banished" from Grenada, imprisoned, tortured and threatened. It was common knowledge in Grenada, and in America, that destabilizers faced "the heavy hand of revolution". Few Grenadians publicly questioned the revolution. Most of the private responses were gotten from Grenadians who were former supporters of the revolution or from members of the P.R.A. who felt that the revolution was moving in the wrong direction.

We found it difficult to get at the real reasons of why the Grenada revolution failed. The public images were presented quite well by members of the P.R.G. and several of our interviewees had problems distinguishing between the private and public images of the revolution. A former Minister in the P.R.G. told the authors that he was confused and simply couldn't explain what happened on October 25, the day of the American intervention. It should be pointed out that several government Ministers of the P.R.G. were not members of the Central Committee, the decision-making body of the N.J.M.

Having dealt with the feelings and meanings of the revolution which are normally taken for granted, we were now prepared to undertake what Jack Douglas would have called self-deceptions. "The self-deceptions are actually conscious feelings and ideas, which are readily available, easily expressed, well verbalized, and advertised to the world. They are the verbal accounts, the self presentations, that the individual gives to the world about things which are vital and fearful to him; but which are in conflict with those deeper, generally unconscious fears. They are also the things he himself believes-he insists on their truth and holds onto them tenaciously, though there are also times when he doubts them and temporarily grasps the underlying fear that inspires the self-deception"[14].

Immediately after Bishop's death, several loyal supporters of the P.R.G. openly criticized the ideologies and directions of the government. Telephone interviews with P.R.G. supporters revealed that many of them supported the politics of the P.R.G. and the N.J.M. for personal gains and social recognition. The revolution afforded several Grenadians in Grenada an opportunity to "fight for a cause". The "revo", as it is locally called, gave the poor and the urban elite an opportunity to assume leadership roles in the Party. Therefore, the P.R.G. supporters were more concerned with protecting their own images and interests than they were with the truth, direction and meaning of the revolution.

Supporters of the revolution who reside overseas supported the movement because it gave them a sense of "peoplehood". Mr. M.S. told the authors that "for the first time in my life I have something that I am really committed to. The 'revo' gave me, and several people like me, a sense of peoplehood. We have a cause that many Grenadians can call their own"[13]. Mr. M.S., a professional engineer, also said that the revolution enabled many Grenadians to return to Grenada and make a contribution. What he did not tell the authors was that his trips to Grenada were personally motivated. Mr. M.S., and others like himself periodically returned to Grenada to "relive their old way of life"[15]. In other words Mr. M.S. was not only returning to "work for the cause", but also "to get a new sense of self-worth". Being a supporter of the P.R.G. guaranteed him a red carpet welcome in Grenada. Telephone interviews with supporters of the P.R.G. found that many supported the revolution for political and not ideological reasons. As a matter of fact, supporters of Bishop are now saying "God bless America", and are returning to Grenada to assume positions with the new government. The hard-core supporters of the revolution are the college educated and the urban elite.

We used a multiplicity of sources to get at the private images and meanings of the revolution. In addition to interviews, newspapers and magazines were extremely helpful. Newspapers and magazines that were opposed to the P.R.G. published negative articles. Those who supported the ideology and direction of the P.R.G. refused to publish anything negative. The ones most helpful to us, were those that simply analyzed the revolution and its role to the rest of the Caribbean nations and to the world in general. Newspapers and magazines that are neutral, when carefully analyzed, depicted the private side of the revolution. We collected articles from magazines and newspapers published in America, England, Canada, Trinidad and Tobago, Grenada, Barbados, Jamaica, St. Lucia, St. Vincent, Dominica and St. Kitts. Articles found in *The New York Times, The New York Daily News, Caribbean Review, Everybody's Magazine, The Miami Herald, The Grenadian Voice, The Jamaican Gleaner, The Trinidad Guardian, The Trinidad Express, The Barbados Advocate, The Vincentian,* and a host of others, were quite helpful. These articles were analytical, usually unbiased, investigative, and pointed.

Personal letters were also quite helpful. We analyzed letters received from friends, relatives, and informants. We agree with W.I. Thomas and Florian Znaniecki when they say that personal life-records constitute the perfect type of sociological material. "If we were forced to use mass phenomena as material, or any kind of happenings taken without regard to the life-histories of the individuals who participate in them, it is a defect, not an advantage, of our present sociological method"[16].

The letters collected enabled us to probe for hidden meanings. Even though the letters did not, in any way, analyze the revolution, they provided us with enough information to understand that the direction of the revolution had changed. On December 30, 1979, Mr. S.C. wrote a letter which stated: "Boy, I really don't know what is happening in Grenada. I cannot tell you exactly what is happening. The only thing I could say is that Grenadians better be careful." This statement by Mr. S.C. should not be seen as a criticism of the revolution. Mr. S.C. knew that the revolution was not progressing as he had envisioned and was, thus, expressing his frustrations. Similar letters were received. An examination of these letters helped us understand the inner workings of the revolution. We used this data to measure attitudes of professionals, religious leaders, and middle and working class Grenadians. It would have been very difficult for us to understand the direction of the revolution without the help of letters that we received. In other words, these letters helped us reach "the actual human experiences and attitudes which constitute the full, live and active social reality beneath the formal organization of social institutions, or behind the statistically tabulated mass-phenomena which taken in themselves are nothing but symptoms of unknown casual processes and can serve only as a provisional ground for sociological hypotheses."[16]

Sociologists who want to arrive at the truth must question the taken-for-granted in everyday life. The public images of the revolution were examples of that which is often taken for granted and, therefore, became one of the central topics of our investigation. It became clearer during the research that the public images of the revolution had very little relationship to social reality. These images were propaganda designed to present a false hope. The contradictions between ideology and reality were carefully managed by members of the P.R.G. A propaganda machinery was developed to deal with individuals who questioned the public images of the revolution. Such individuals were labeled destabilizers, Gairyites, Capitalists, Federal Bureau of Investigation (FBI) informants, Central Intelligence Agency (CIA) spies, and disloyal Grenadians. Personal attacks were made against so-called destabilizers, and individuals who opposed the revolution were beaten, threatened, imprisoned, killed, and slandered.

Our task, therefore, was to penetrate and describe the hidden meanings. In order to do this, we searched for what Robert Patrick, Everett Hughes and Irving Goffman might have called hidden dramatic structures. "From a dramatic standpoint, the central problem of a community sociologist is to achieve an objective perspective that encompasses the partial perspectives held by various groups in the community in such a fashion as to call attention to hidden processes without losing sight of the meanings of the various partial perspectives."[9]

We were also faced with the problem of confronting changing human dramas. These included changing ideologies, values, suspicion, and images. We got around this dilemma by always trying to find out the point of view of how the social actors defined the revolution. We looked for the relationship between the individual's consciousness and his wider social reality-between action and structure.

## Organization of the Study.

Chapter One describes the political, economical, religious, familial and educational structure of Grenada. Chapter Two looks at Gairy's administration and the emergence of the N.J.M. Chapter Three presents a chronology of the Grenada revolution. Chapter Four looks at the ideology of the movement. Chapter Five examines the leadership of the Grenada revolution. Chapter Six interprets the revolution and presents a sociological analysis of why it failed.

# CHAPTER ONE

# GRENADA: A SOCIO-ECONOMIC

# AND POLITICAL HISTORY

Grenada was first sighted by Columbus in 1498, but the first attempt to colonize the island did not occur until 1609. Partially because of the harassment of settlers by the original inhabitants of the islands, the Caribs, a permanent settlement was not established until 1650, when the Caribs ceded the islands to the French West Indian Company. In 1651 the French slaughtered most of the Caribs. From 1674 to 1763 Grenada was controlled by the French. The French lost control of the island to the British in 1763. The island was recaptured by the French in 1779. It was permanently ceded to England by the Treaty of Versailles in 1783.

The Treaty of Versailles did not end the feuding between England and France for possession of Grenada. By 1795 the French Republic made a strong attempt to regain Grenada by bringing about an insurrection of the French inhabitants and slaves. The French accused the British of giving their churches to the Crown.

On March 2, 1795, the French General Fedon and his men, mainly freemen and slaves from the French and English plantations, attacked Grenville, located on the eastern coast of the island. Except for St. George's, Fedon's forces gained control of most of the island. Fearing a new Haiti, the British authorities sent 200 men under the command of Gen. Ralph Abercromby to reinforce its troops. Fedon's troops were forced to yield their positions until they were finally defeated at Mount Qua Qua. Fedon escaped and was never captured, but most of the ringleaders were sentenced to death on grounds of high treason, while the rest were deported to Honduras.

"These, then, were the main results and implications of the rebellion of 1795: a crippled island economy, severe property destruction for British whites, confiscation of the estates of the insurrectionists, and loss of life both in terms of those killed in action and execution of convicted

14

insurgents... , Fedon's rebellion demonstrated that Grenada's free coloreds and slaves were not satisfied with the existing social conditions and were prepared to do something about them.

Grenada, commonly called the isle of spice, is located ninety miles northeast of the Caribbean Island of Trinidad. It lies at 12 degrees north latitude and 61 degrees west longitude. The total area of the island is approximately 133 square miles, and it has a population of 110,000 people.[2] The beauty of the island lies in its rugged broken surfaces. Most of the island is about 1000 feet above sea level. The highest point is Mount Saint Catherine which is 2,750 feet high. The island is divided into six parishes - St. Andrew, St. George, St. Mark, St. John, St. David, and St. Patrick. The capital of Grenada is St. George's which is also the seat of the island's political government and the home of the majority of the elite.

The climate is tropical with the average temperature falling in the low eighties, except from November to January when the weather is somewhat cooler. Soils are of the red, red-brown, yellow-brown, and gray varieties, reflecting their volcanic origin.[3] The soil is not ideal for agriculture but with the help of pen manure, compost, and artificial fertilizer, it produces fairly good crops.

**The Economic Structure of Grenada**

The majority of the population were slaves, and sugar was the main export crop. Emancipation, in 1838, brought about a distaste for regular labor on the sugar plantation. The freed slaves became interested in cultivating their own gardens in the interior of the island. The cultivation of laborers' gardens on the highest elevations led to the introduction of cocoa planting, an industry better suited to both the soil and terrain of Grenada. In 1848 nutmeg was introduced. The sugar planters were not of course easily reconciled to the introduction of new crops and imported laborers from Malta and Portugal. By 1849 over 1000 freed slaves were imported on contract. After their contracts ended, the majority of them became landowners or squatters like their predecessors. The gradual transference of the island from sugar to cocoa and nutmeg began with Emancipation and in 1856 no less than 47 sugar estates had been abandoned and nine others were on the eve of change.

Cocoa, nutmeg, bananas, and spices comprise the bulk of the island's exports. Bananas were introduced to Grenada in 1954 and are presently the number one export. Nutmeg is the second export in value. Cocoa is the third, and is noted overseas for its high quality.₄ Copra and sugar are minor export products. Carriacou produces limes, peanuts, cotton, and is also known for boat building.

The agricultural land covers 82 percent of the island's territory, the productive land about 65 percent. In 1968, 63 percent of all exports went to Britain. Since even peasant farmers are mainly interested in cultivation for export, Grenada is dependent on food imports which head the list of imports by a wide margin.

The distribution of land is very uneven in Grenada. A few wealthy plantation owners own most of the land. The 1946 census showed that there were some 69,000 acres of land on the island, four thousand acres (4,000) were occupied by the government as forest reserve. "One hundred and sixteen parcels of more than 100 acres accounted for 40,000 acres, while the remainder fell into 200 units between 20 and 100 acres each,1,200 units of 5 to 20 acres, 4,900 holdings of 1 to 5 acres and 4,800 plots of less than 1 acre each."₅ This system of land distribution has not changed very much since 1946. Ex-Prime Minister Eric Matthew Gairy initiated a program in 1974 to correct the uneven distribution of land. The program, "Land for the Landless", was not very successful. The intent of the program was not achieved. The redistribution of land to the masses was criticized and rejected by the opposition.

The economic wealth of the island is also unevenly distributed. Wealth is centered on land, import and export trades, and manufacturing. There are few instances of self-made millionaires. Wealth in Grenada is not usually an individual accomplishment but a family privilege. Within the rigid stratification system, wealth is carefully guarded since access to wealth could lead to a questioning of the class system. Endogamy, skin color, family name, and geographical location are factors that are used to maintain the rigid stratification system. The old aristocratic families and their off-spring who are predominantly whites, continue to control the wealth of the country. Wealth, power, prestige, status, and honor are associated with skin color. Most of the landed aristocrats, the large import/export merchants and the large manufacturers are mulattos. A sprinkling of East Indians can also be found in this category.₆

**The Grenadian Family Structure**

In Grenada the man is "lord and master" of this household. His roles are clearly specified. He provides for his family, and protects them from physical harm and malicious slander. Raymond T. Smith captured this well when he said that "a man with any pride cannot see his wife and children inadequately housed or fed, nor can he allow others to take advantage of them without taking the offender to court".[7]

In Grenada the man is the authority figure. His authority and "manhood" is seldom questioned. Women who question the authority of their husbands are seen as wanting "to take away the pants from their husbands". Judith Blake, in her book entitled *Family Structure In Jamaica,* said that "a man must be master in his household if he is married".[8] Weak household heads are called "sissies", "insecures", and "mamas boys". Needless to say that the situation in Jamaica is similar to that in Grenada.

The traditional culture that exists on the island controls the relationship between husband and wife. The upper class woman obeys her husband because of societal pressures. The majority of upper class Grenadian women do not work and depend on their husbands for the entire upkeep of the household. In addition to this, the middle and upper class women are expected to love and obey their husbands.

Like the upper and middle class women, lower class women also respect the authority of their mates. This respect is derived from both cultural and physical expectations. Lower class women who refuse to obey their mates are physically beaten. Physical force is used by lower class men to keep their women in their places. Wife beatings are tolerated if they are used to protect the integrity of men. In other words, wife beatings are acceptable when the man is publicly insulted by his woman.[6]

The Grenadian family structure, to a very large extent, has maintained some of its African traditions. "Within Hausa homes, relations are highly formal. Men remain in the forecourt when they are at home and have little to do with the domestic round. Emphasis on life-long monogamy is equally essential."[9]

## The Family and Political Socialization

In Grenada, as in most other Caribbean countries, politics is viewed as a dirty game. The old upper classes encourage their children to stay out of politics. The middle classes, especially the new middle classes, see politics as a means to legitimate power and upward mobility. The N.J.M. which was made up of the sons and daughters of the new middle class saw their involvement in politics as a means to social advancement.

The lower classes seldom enter politics for personal gains. Those who participate in the political process do so for emotional reasons. For example, "lower class women often take a strong interest in partisan politics and tend to be more emotionally committed to parties and political personalities..'[10]. Grenadians support politicians that are emotionally and socially appealing. Gairy's support, as mentioned earlier, came from the lower classes.

His opposition came from the upper and new middle class. The problem of the new middle class was to find political and social identity. The fact that they were lawyers, economists, doctors, professors or teachers did not guarantee them access to the political hierarchy of Grenada. The new middle class considered itself as educationally and culturally superior to the culture and traditions of lower class Grenadians. The lower class accused the elite class of snobbishness, of being "uncle toms", and of trying to force its "reform politics" on Grenadians.[11] The new middle class interest in politics was not for the good of the working class but instead to promote their own self-interest and to avoid entering professional work. "Their interest in politics, then, represents some search for ideals and for meaningful activity which is otherwise denied."[11]

The new elite saw themselves as the ones who were best prepared to run Grenada. Preparation to them meant having college and professional degrees. The lower class was not as impressed as the elite with college diplomas. Instead, they supported individuals who were chosen by Gairy. Archibald Singham captured the situation well when he said that "middle class women interviewed tended to be quite vocal in their opposition to Gairy, whom they obviously perceived as a threat to their way of life. One middle-class family in which both husband and wife were brown, characterized Gairy as a typical black rabble-rouser who had no manners. In all the families interviewed... the children seemed to be essentially indifferent to politics, generally accepting their parents evaluation about the personalities of the leaders".[10] The lower class, on the other hand saw Gairy as a good man who is "for us black people".

The statement that Gairy was a black rabble-rouser should not be taken at face value but must be carefully analyzed. "The lower class man... is much more hostile toward both the white and brown elites, and sees in them the reason for his misery..."[10] Gairy, at least originally, represented the interest of this class. He gave them a voice in the political process of Grenada. Needless to say, the elite class and the administration, the Queen's representative, never accepted Gairy's authority and did everything in their power to discredit his rule.

The March 13th revolution can therefore be viewed as a struggle by the lower class against the upper class and the new middle class. The revolution was an instrument used by the latter to regain the political power it lost in 1951. This thesis will be fully explored and developed in a later chapter.

**The Political Structure Of Grenada**

Unlike the Leeward Islands and British Honduras, Grenada became a Crown Colony by acts of the Imperial Parliament of England. The Treaty of Paris established a "Government of Grenada". Immediately after the Treaty of Paris in 1763, the parliamentary system known as the old Representative System was granted by Royal Proclamation to Grenada. This system was based on the British constitution in its classical seventeenth-century form. The governor who represented the crown had executive control while parliament was responsible for legislation. It should be pointed out that the parliament or nominated council was an advisory body and had very little executive power. This arrangement was not always acceptable to the majority of Grenadians since it was a form of "taxation without representation". Singham said that "assemblies in the Caribbean had the reputation of being tenacious, quarrelsome and obscure. From their inception the assemblies in the Windwards clashed with the governor... The first Grenada Assembly, meeting in 1766, was dissolved within a few weeks, after a controversy with the governor over a claim to adjourn without his consent..."[10] The new House of Assembly faced additional problems. To counteract the problems of political rights from Roman Catholics, they "limit the powers of the assemblies in the ceded islands, and the governor relied heavily on imperial disallowance of legislations."[10]

The abolition of slavery in 1834 and the abolition of the apprentice system in 1838 dealt a severe blow to the Old Representative System. After slavery, the ex-slaves who acquired the necessary qualifications were allowed to vote. The abolition of slavery also led to several labor shortages on sugar plantations. The droughts in the 1840's and the Act of the British Parliament equalizing duties on British and foreign sugar led to a serious decline in sugar prices. The drop in revenue greatly underminded the Assembly's power. By the 1860's the colonial office finally decided to turn all the islands under the Old Representative System into crown colonies. This change occured in Grenada in 1875. The final step was the abolition of these legislatures and the imposition of pure crown colony government which transformed the legislative council into an entirely nominated body. In 1879 Grenada received full Crown Colony Government. The Executive Council consisted of the governor, 13 officials, 7 non-officials nominated by the governor, and 3 other officials nominated by the governor. From 1879 onward the island was completely controlled by the governor and his elected "cabinet". T.A. Marryshow, commonly known as the father of the West-Indian Federation, protested against the Executive council form of government and petitioned the Secretary of State in Westminister for elected representatives. By 1920 tempers ran high in St. George's, and there was an attempt to burn the city.

The Wood Commission visited the Caribbean in 1922. This Commission was sent to the Caribbean to examine the structure of government that existed on the island. In 1924 the Wood Commission recommended that a semi-representative system be introduced. This new system was comprised of elected and unofficial members. The governor, under the new system, continued to have the deciding vote. This arrangement did not quite satisfy Marryshow and his supporters who demanded that "The West Indies must be West Indian" and "Crown Colony rule must go".

## The 1936 Constitution

The 1936 Constitution[12] represented the beginning of a change in emphasis under Crown Colony government from the nominated and ex-officio element in the legislative council to the elected element, although control was still vested firmly in the hands of the executive. "For the first time the elected members were equal in number to the ex-officio and nominated combine. However, this was counterbalanced by giving the governor reserved powers, which he could use to certify a bill in the Executive Council even though the legislature had rejected it, and which were subsequently used in Grenada..." [10]

The 1936 Constitution was not satisfactory to the small group of Grenadians who were politically conscious. They saw the new arrangement as essentially a Crown Colony system wherein the executive remained responsible to the crown. Between 1934 and 1938 there were widespread strikes in most of the islands. The resulting factor was the development of trade unions. In order to deal with the existing problems, several commissions were appointed. The Royal Commission, better known as the Moyne Commission, rejected complete self-government based on universal suffrage on the grounds that it would make financial control by Britian impossible.

The Windward Islands Conference held in Grenada proposed adult suffrage for literates, a reduction in official voting power, an increase in elected membership, and a federal legislature for the windwards. After much debate and political maneuvers, the Secretary of State, in 1949, accepted the idea of adult suffrage, subject to a literacy test. [13]

The year 1951 can be described as a political milestone for the Windward Islands. During this year some constitutional reforms were granted. "Universal adult suffrage was granted without qualifications. Membership in the Legislative Council became open to any British subject over 21 residing in the colony, with an ability to speak, read, and understand English to a degree sufficient to enable him to take an active part in the proceedings of the council... The third major change was that for the first time since the abolition of the Old Representative System there was to be a clear majority of elected members in the legislature... And at last an attempt was made to deal with that longstanding source of friction: the overlapping of the functions of the legislature and the executive..." [10] :

The constitution, while being a major improvement over the Old Representative System, contained several parts that were not in the best interest of Grenadians who were determined to control their own destiny. For example, the elected members on the Executive were still in a minority and could not effectively control the council without the support of at least one of the official members. The new constitution did not severely limit the autocratic power of the governor. He was empowered by the

Rc yal Instructions to ignore the Executive council "if he shall in any case consider it right to do so." [14] Clause 26 of the legislative council's report (1951) gave the governor full control over the islands' finances.

The 1951 constitution, even though it recognized the strength of mass organization, made no provisions for their involvement in the exercise of power. The powers that the 1951 constitution talked about were titular and not actual power.

### Constitutional Developments In Grenada In The 1950's

In February 1956 the islands of the Caribbean decided to federate. The Federal Constitution provided for a federal Government General and a federal Prime Minister. The constitution called for an upper house consisting of two senators from each participating territory, [15] and a lower house which was to be elected by popular representation.

One of the major problems of Federal Constitution was that the smaller islands did not have constitutional parity with the larger islands of Jamaica and Trinidad. At a meeting on Constitutional reform held in Trinidad in 1959, it was decided that the territories of the Leeward and Windward Islands should be allowed to manage their own affairs, and that the Executive Council should be controlled by the legislature and not be the Governor-General. The members further insisted that each island should have its own Premier. At a similar conference held in London it was agreed that the leader of the government in the legislative council would be entitled Chief Minister. It was also decided at the London Conference that general elections should be held in each territory. This proposal gave rise to a ministerial form of government for Grenada.

Under the agreements of the 1959 Constitution, the Administrator was to appoint the Chief Minister, to constitute offices and make appointments, to appoint, control and discipline the Public Service, and to maintain law and order. "The powers of the Administrator were considerable in spite of the 'advanced' nature of the constitution, although in a number of areas his role tended to be somewhat vague or to overlap others. One of the major difficulties of his position was that he was accountable to three bodies: the Secretary of State for the Colonies, the federal financial officials, and the legislature of Grenada. Nonetheless, he was still, in the words of the famous Colonial Regulation 105, the single and supreme authority responsible to, and representative of, Her Majesty." [16] The existence of two executive offices created conflicts. These conflicts led to the suspension of the constitution in 1962. After the elections of September 1962, the 1959 constitution was restored. The amended constitution gave the administrator wider discretionary powers. He now had the right to appoint the Minister of Finance if he saw fit. The amended document also meant that the Adminstrator could appoint high-level civil servants or members of the Public Service Commission (P.S.C.) without consulting the Prime Minister. Singham was correct when he said that Grenada, in 1962, was less constitutionally advanced than the other countries in the Leeward and Windward islands that were not self-governing. The system of government could be considered non-functional at best.

As late as 1962, half of the members of the District Boards were appointed by the Administrator, who was not required to consult with the Prime Minister in making these appointments. "To be elected, an individual must have an income of at least $250 per annum; own property worth $960; be a registerd barrister, doctor or clergyman... The strong class bias of these requirements is unmistakable, thus denying the peasantry or legitimate politicians from the 'wrong' class any chance to exercise even limited power in their local communities..."[10]

Several attempts were made to reform the system of local government found in Grenada. E.S. Christiani recommended that a central, cohesive administrative body be created. The structure, the local Government Board, was to consist of central government officials and representative of all the district boards. In 1956 a select committee called for the creation of "local government councils which would be directly responsible to the minister responsible for local government."[10] The legislative council did not act on these proposals.

The administrator enjoyed what Weber characterized as institutional charisma. He exercised authority because he represented the legal power structure and because of his position (office) as representative of the Queen of England. The rest of this chapter will look at the political and economical situations that existed in Grenada prior to 1951.

As mentioned earlier, the acquisition of land by former slaves led to the creation of a large landed peasantry. These small plots were economical but the freed slaves soon became disenchanted and disgruntled. To supplement their income, some small land owners worked two or three days a week on the large plantations. Up to the 1950's, therefore, the economic situation in Grenada was such that all sectors of the population had good reason to be dissatisfied. Economic depression was felt in many quarters. Many Grenadians emigrated to Trinidad, Aruba,

England and the United States. The wars of 1914-18 and 1939-45 did little to alleviate the suffering that Grenadians experienced.

The working conditions on the estates were deplorable. The large land owners were mainly concerned about the output of labor from the workers. Men received 54¢ per day and women about 42¢ daily. The decades of the thirties and forties were trying ones for large landowners, peasant farmers, and estate laborers. While there were strikes and threats of strikes in neighboring Caribbean islands, there was no effective trade union to fight for the causes of the estate workers in Grenada.

However, in the early forties, E.A. Mitchell formed the Grenada Workers Union (G.W.U.) which catered to clerical and city workers. The estates workers, who formed the largest number of the laborers, were not represented by the G.W.U.. These agricultural workers who were overworked, underpaid, and underrepresented looked for a leader who could change their economic and social conditions. In 1950, Eric Matthew Gairy appeared on the scene, and the workers suddenly found an individual who was willing and able to champion their cause. "By the end of the 1940's, 87 percent of the houses in Grenada were still wood, wattle and mud; 80 percent were either one or two room dwellings with absolutely no privacy for adults."[16]

The Grenada Manual and Mental Workers Union (G.M.M.W.U.) was organized by Gairy and this organization was the match which ignited the discontent that had been simmering for decades among Grenadian peasants and workers. "Up to that time the workers were represented by two trade unions, the St. John's Labor Party (S.J.L.P.) and the G.W.U. By 1950 these unions came to be viewed as almost synonymous with the employers of labor in attitudes, values and beliefs, even by the very workers they represented."[18] Gairy's resentment to this type of social arrangement led him to challenge the elite structure of government that he found in Grenada.

# CHAPTER TWO

# THE RISE AND FALL OF

# ERIC MATTHEW GAIRY

The economical, social, and political conditions that existed in Grenada led to massive unrest among the workers and peasant farmers. On the one hand, the peasants were dissatisfied because they felt that Britain was not doing enough to promote their products. On the other hand, they were dissatisfied with their social living conditions. In many instances, the conditions of the peasants were not much better than those experienced during slavery.

In 1949 Gairy returned to Grenada and immediately challenged the establishment and the large landowners. He was viewed by the peasants as a charismatic leader, a person sent by God to relieve them of their bondage. He was "considered extraordinary and treated as endowed with supernatural, superhuman, or at least specifically exceptional powers or qualities."[1]

Unlike T.A. Marryshow or "Doc" Mitchell, Gairy enjoyed islandwide support. In 1951, Gairy's G.U.L.P. won the national election by a landslide, winning six of the eight elected seats. The people's hero, after two years as a trade union leader, had become a professional politician. In two years, he achieved what no other leader had been able to achieve. Coming from the rank and file of the "grass roots" he knew first hand the problems, needs, aims, and desires of the working class.

Gairy was born in 1922 in the parish of St. Andrew's. Unable to attend one of the local secondary schools, he left Grenada at the age of twenty to seek employment in the oil fields of Trinidad. From Trinidad he migrated to Aruba and worked in the refinery. While in Aruba he attended literary classes and became involved in political trade unionism.

Gairy's return to Grenada in 1949 opened a new era of hope: "An era when for the first time the 'crowd' was about to enter the political stage.

No longer did the people feel themselves to be the audience, the lookers-on, they considered themselves the actors, the participants in the play, which was written, produced and directed by the 'hero' himself - Eric Gairy.''[2] He understood the Grenadian peasant culture quite well and simply gave them what they wanted. Gairy became an expert at "impression management.''[3] In other words, Gairy's actions were designed to convey impressions that were beneficial to him. He also managed the behaviors of all members of his political team. He understood that it was "crucial for the maintenance of the team's performance that each member of the team possess dramaturgical discipline and exercise it in presenting his own part.''[3] Impression management requires that "actual affective response must be concealed and an appropriate affective response must be displayed.''[3] Every elaborate show that had to be staged in Grenada, was staged by Gairy.

Approximately one month after registering the G.M.M.W.U. in July 1950, Gairy made his first wage demand. He demanded a 50 percent wage increase for workers at the Grenada Sugar Factory. When his demands were not met, he called a strike. The August 24 strike mushroomed and within days workers on eleven agricultural estates walked off their jobs to demonstrate their sympathy for the sugar workers. Gairy seized this opportunity to request a 20 percent wage hike for the agricultural workers. The employers ignored his demands and instead negotiated with the Grenada Trade Union Council (G.T.U.C.) headed by Doc Mitchell. On February 20, 1951, Gairy called a general strike. This strike laid the foundation for Gairy's successful political career.

On February 21, 1951, Gairy's famous mass demonstration was held outside York House while parliament was in session. The demonstration clearly outlined the class differences that existed in Grenada. The thousands of people who came to St. George's on the day of the demonstration represented the lower echelons of Grenadian society. They demonstrated their solidarity by singing "Gairy's National Anthem". It goes something like this: "we will never let our leader fall because we love him the best of all; we will fight, fight, fight to save our rights. . . Because we love him the best of all. . .''

The opposition and resentment to the strikes and demonstrations came from the merchants, store clerks, the civil servants, and the "middle class society of black climbers, brown upper-lips and whites who did not really make it to the St. George's Club.''[2] These individuals saw Gairy as upsetting the existing class structure and of helping "those country folks".

The demonstration brought to the surface the pent up hostilities that existed between the residents of the city and those of the countryside. The St. George's middle class has always had a deep rooted sense of superiority over the working class. They felt threatened and insulted to have their power and authority challenged by the working class. The white colonial establishment which the middle and upper classes respected and cherished was, for the first time, seriously challenged by "country folks". D. Sinclair Dabreo said that the St. George's middle class "envied the workers who were able to unite themselves under one leader and make demands upon the establishment. Demands which they themselves would have been happy to make, were it not for the hypocrisy of the pride of their very way of life, and the fact they had an inexplicable love-hate relationship with their master, be they Establishment Colonials or merchants "[2] The middle classes wanted to become members of the colonial establishment but were prevented from doing so because of racial discrimination, financial costs, skin color, geographical location, and family name.

The demonstration also annoyed the upper classes, the planters, the acting governor, members of parliament and other elected and appointed members of government. The established hierarchy was simply not ready for a leader with Gairy's charismatic and personal charm. His charisma threatened the very existence and values of the colonial system. Gairy's insistence of having an audience with the acting governor infuriated the status quo.

Gairy used his skill as a social actor to its fullest. Dressed in a mixture of sports and evening wear, his walking stick and his broad and friendly smiles, he promised the masses better working conditions, higher wages and personal self-respect. He intimated that he might be arrested but insisted that they remain firm and committed to the cause.

Gairy's ability as an actor, coupled with his charismatic leadership posed a serious problem to the establishment. To ignore him would incite the demonstrators. To grant him his requests would undermine the existing political and social structure. On the other hand, it was impossible to ignore his presence and pretend that he did not exist.

How would the acting governor deal with Gairy and his loyal supporters? The acting governor finally decided to put Gairy and his top advisor on a British gunboat and ship them to nearby Carriacou. This action on the part of the acting governor was quite symbolic and paid off well for Gairy. Gairy boasted afterwards that he had to be taken away from his people, because the establishment was afraid of him and his followers. The little, poor, black man from the country had won the day.

From February 23, to March 6 terror reigned supreme throughout the entire country. There were burnings and lootings and his supporters called for the release of Gairy. In desperation, after days of increased burning and looting, the governor asked Gairy for his assistance in putting an end to the violence. On March 8, 1951, Gairy appeared on radio to appeal to his supporters to stop the violence. In that speech he told his supporters to return to work on March 9, and immediately stop the burning of buildings and fields. This appeal was obeyed by the strikers. In return for their cooperation, they were given a considerable increase in pay. At age 29 Gairy became the undisputed leader of the trade union movement in Grenada.

Gairy turned his popularity as a union leader into political power. He was elected to political office in 1951. Nevertheless, he was unable to turn his charisma as a union leader into political charisma. When the 1951 crisis ended his charismatic leadership slowly disappeared. The strict limits of the political system stiffled his apparent power. Gairy's refusal to register his union accounts, and his insistence on not paying his driver's license fees placed him in direct conflict with the laws of Grenada. In the 1951 election, G.U.L.P. won 71 percent of the votes. By 1954, the percentage was down to 54. In 1957 the G.U.L.P. won only 2 seats. On October 28, 1957, Gairy lost his franchise and his seat in parliament. This loss of his franchise did not prevent him from exercising political control on the politics of Grenada.

In the 1961 elections he supported his hand-picked candidate, Joshua Thorne. Gairy's party, the G.U.L.P. won eight of the ten seats. George Clyne was appointed Chief Minister. The results of the 1961 elections demonstrated that Gairy had strong support in Grenada. On July 24, 1961, a by-election was held. Gairy won handsomely and in August he became Chief Minister. These turn of events did not end Gairy's troubles as a political leader.

On June 7, 1962, a Commission of Inquiry was appointed by James Lloyd, the Queen's representative in Grenada, to examine the accounts of public expenditures of Gairy from January 1, 1961. The Commission's reported findings were a slap in Gairy's face. The Squandamania Report challenged Gairy's credibility as an honest and capable leader. To complicate matters for him, the Commission's findings stated that there were financial abuses. The findings of this report led to the suspension of Grenada's constitution and the giving to an administrator all executive powers. As expected, the members of the G.U.L.P., the working classes and residents of the countryside supported Gairy and claimed that the Squandamania Report was an attempt by England and upper class Grenadians to discredit Gairy. The supporters of Gairy further argued that James Lloyd, and enemy of Gairy, was bent on removing their leader from office. In this atmosphere of political turmoil and uncertainty the administrator set 1962 as the date for new elections.

Two major issues surfaced during the 1962 campaign. They are "Squandamania" and the "Go Trinidad Movement". The Grenada National Party (G.N.P.), a party that represented the interests of the middle and upper classes, used the Squandamania issue to discredit Gairy. The supporters of the G.N.P. accepted this while the supporters of the G.U.L.P. viewed this move as a ploy to remove their leader from office. The "Go Trinidad" idea became the thing that all Grenadians talked about. Many Grenadians felt that Grenada, after the breakup of the Federation in 1962, had more to gain by joining with Trinidad and Tobago. Gairy, after superficial discussions with Dr. Eric Williams, the late Prime Minister of Trinidad and Tobago, opted to continue negotiations with Barbados and six other Caribbean states in an attempt to form a mini-federation. Gairy told the electorates in 1962 that he was still prepared to consider the "Go Trinidad" idea. The electorates did not believe him. Gairy was accused of maintaining his own self esteem and preferred not to have to play second fiddle to anyone. A poem published in *The West Indian* newspaper depicted Gairy as "playing smart". The poem reads as follows:

> Come early or come late
> Uncle is for 'Little Eight'
> But Uncle knows that Trinidad
> Is what will make Grenada glad
>
> 'Little Eight' is Uncle's pet
> Because that's where he's sure to get
> Motor car and house and ting
> Plenty cash for him to fling
>
> So Uncle said in his usual style
> 'My dear people wait a while

After election I will show
Which way Grenada is to go'

Uncle feels he's playing smart
'Little Eight' is in his heart
Some say, so now kill we a goat
He couldn't get a high vote

But now he finds the pressure hard
The people voting Trinidad
So Uncle said 'You have to see
Williams will only talk to me'

But Uncle been and talk before
And what happened? What's the score?
Williams and I can't agree
Grenada will lose her identity

If you see we put Gairy back
That will be his same attack
Make as if for Unitary State
Then sell us out to 'Little Eight'

Gairy was in trouble and he knew it. He had simply misunderstood the close ties that exist between Grenada and Trinidad. For the first time since he returned to Grenada in 1949, his leadership and his ability to "manage impressions" were challenged. To counteract his loss of charismatic leadership, Gairy accused those who opposed him as "Judases", false prophets. On the night before the elections, "Gairy entered the Carenage (or Inner Harbour) in St. George's on a vessel coming like the Biblical Shepherd to address his sheep..."[2] The meeting, as usual, commenced with the lighting of candles and the uttering of the Lord's Prayer. The meeting ended with Gairy lambasting his opposition.

This last minute feat of showmanship was not sufficient to stop the inroads that the G.N.P. made earlier in the campaign. The results of the election in 1962 gave the G.N.P. a 6 to 4 victory over the G.U.L.P., Gairy's party. The results of this election undermined Gairy's leadership. Several Grenadians said openly that Gairy might have sinned and therefore lost favor with God. A staunch supporter of Gairy told the authors that "Gairy loves women and might have used some of our government money to support his mistresses. As a man of God, he should live up to the Master's wishes. I still respect him but he needs to change his ways."₄ Another person told us that the loss of the election was God's signal to Gairy. While his charisma was challenged and questioned, he nevertheless remained a popular leader.

The G.N.P. was not successful in establishing political links with Trinidad. Gairy, once he realized that there would be no Unitary State, called for the resignation of H.A. Blaize, the then Premier, and leader of the G.N.P., and the other members of the party. He accused the G.N.P. of plotting with the old English aristocracy to remove him from office. In the 1967 election he reminded the electorates of this and insisted that they return him and his party to office. He also reminded the working classes that the G.N.P. was comprised of the "big shots", those who exploited the workers. Gairy understood the culture and values of the electorates and used them to their fullest. Phrases like "town and country", "rich and poor", "the people's leader", "the small man's leader", and "God's servant" were used constantly throughout the 1967 campaign. Gairy's attack on the G.N.P. for its inabilities to achieve a Unitary State worked well for him. He won the election handsomely.

Gairy's invincibility as a leader was nevertheless challenged. The crisis of 1951 was over and with it Gairy's charisma. He demanded obedience in 1951 because he was constantly able to "prove" himself. He met and even surpassed the expectations of most of the workers. He secured for them better working conditions, higher wages, self respect and self-esteem and, above all, the ability for them to question the value, culture, and authority of the upper classes. The children of the 1951 workers were adults in 1961 and they too had hopes, dreams and aspirations that were markedly different from those of their parents. Not only did the new generation question the authority of the upper classes, they were also bent on changing it. Most of this new breed saw Gairy as an obstacle to progress. They accused him of being old fashioned, and a puppet of the old English aristocrats. The younger generation accused Gairy of corruption, routinization and ineffective leadership.

By 1967 Gairy was unable to perform heroic deeds. Weber was correct when he said that "the charismatic leader gains and maintains authority solely by proving his strength in life. If he wants to be a prophet, he must perform miracles; if he wants to be a war lord, he must perform heroic deeds. Above all, however, his divine mission must 'prove' itself in that those who faithfully surrender to him must fare well. If they do not fare well, he is obviously not the master sent by the gods."₅

In 1951 Gairy stood outside the framework of the existing political power structure. By 1967, he represented the power structure. Max Weber said that "in order to do justice to their mission, the holders of charisma, the master as well as his disciples and followers, must stand outside the ties of this world, outside the routine occupations, as well as outside the routine obligations of family life..."₅

Gairy's claim that he was sent by God to rule Grenada could no longer guarantee his political survival. He knew that in order to maintain political power on the island, he had to formalize his rule. "In order to maintain his control of Grenada, Gairy, out of necessity, surrounded himself with a formalized structure of bureaucracy. He composed his bureaucracy using trusted friends and associates who shared his ideology. These people were willing to carry out the policies of Gairy's new government - without questions."₇

Any form of opposition was silenced by Gairy. Civil servants who dared question his rule and authority were dealt with forthwith. Political victimization, the method most frequently used against disloyal civil servants, meant dismissal, transfer, or rather exile in remote places.₈ Several of the disloyal workers were beaten.

His government also passed "a series of repressive laws like the Firearms Act (F.A.) (1968) which rescinded all firearms permits issued to members of the opposition; the Public Order Act (P.O.A.) (1974) which banned the use of loudspeakers not previously authorized by police; the Newspaper Act (N.A.) (1975) which required a deposit of 20,000 Eastern Caribbean Dollars (E.C.D.). . . to be made prior to any newspaper being authorized to circulate, and which was obviously directed against the N.J.M. publication; the Essential Public Services Act (E.P.S.C.) and the Port Authority Act (P.A.A.) whereby the right to strike was virtually prohibited in these sectors."₈ Clearly, these repressive laws were designed to suppress and even intimidate that sector of the Grenadian citizenry that was not supportive of the Gairy regime.

The political victimization of the civil servants and harrassment and arrest by the police of individuals who opposed Gairy's rule were not enough to put an end to the growing opposition. The Mongoose Gang first came to public notice during the G.U.L.P. campaign in the 1967 elections. This gang of convicted felons, henchmen, and badmen became Gairy's personal body guards. They acted as a type of secret police and dealt harshly with Gairy's opponents. The primary function of the Mongoose Gang was to act on behalf of Gairy: to silence by sheer force those who opposed or blasphemed him. During its reign, the Mongoose

Gang committed dozens of murders and maimed hundreds of Grenadians all in the name of maintaining this alleged dictator in political office.

Surely, the popularity Gairy initially enjoyed with the Grenadian masses was not to be accorded him forever. His rash behavior, lack of statesmanship, unscrupulous and politically corrupt ways, as well as his vigilantism, culminated in alienating the Grenadian masses from him. More importantly, they demanded that he be removed from political office. One of the Gairy's main political opponents to emerge during this period was a young lawyer named Maurice Bishop. But who exactly was Bishop? And how did he emerge as an alleged charismatic figure who eventually championed the causes of the Grenadian masses in their fight against Gairy between 1970 and 1979?

## Maurice Bishop: The Man

Maurice Rupert Bishop, former Prime Minister of Grenada and also Minister of External Affairs, Information, Culture, Security and Home Affairs, was born in Grenada on May 29, 1944. The son of Rupert and Alimenta Bishop, Bishop spent part of his infancy in Aruba.[9] In 1951, however, when Bishop was seven years old, his family returned to Grenada.[9]

As a young man, Bishop received his early education at both the Wesley Hall Primary School and later at the St. George's Roman Catholic School. He received his High School education at Presentation College. In 1962, while at Presentation, Bishop was awarded the Principal's Gold Medal for outstanding academic achievement and all-around ability.[10] Bishop was also the President of the Student's Union, President and Founding member of the High School's Historical Society, Editor of the school's newspaper, and President of the Debating Society.[10]

In 1963, Bishop graduated from High School with academic honors. After having completed his secondary education, "he co-founded the 'Grenada Assembly of Youth after Truth', an organization aimed at raising the consciousness of youth in his country."[10] Later that year, Bishop left Grenada for London to pursue his intended goal of becoming a lawyer. While in England, he read for a degree in Law at London University. After three years of study, Bishop, in 1966, graduated as a lawyer. That same year he married Angela Redhead who was in Britain pursuing a nursing career. The union produced two children, John and Nadie.[9]

While in England, Bishop was actively involved in public service activities. He was co-founder of the Legal Aid Clinic (L.A.C.) in Nottinghill Gate, President of the West Indian Students Society (W.I.S.S.) at his university, and was a member of an organization named Campaign Against Racial Discrimination (C.A.R.D.).[10]

In 1970 Bishop returned to his native Grenada and went into private practice as a lawyer. He also quickly assumed the role of a leading political spokesperson for the oppressed and poor in both Grenada and the Caribbean region as a whole. In 1970, when "Black Power" was a hot issue in the Caribbean, a number of Grenadians were arrested in Black Power demonstrations in neighboring Trinidad. Bishop subsequently organized rallies and demonstrations protesting the arrest of the Grenadian "Brothers" by the Trinidadian authorities. At this time, Bishop, along with a number of nurses, vehemently protested against unhealthy and deteriorating conditions at the St. George's General Hospital and was later arrested by the police.

This arrest, however, did not deter him from challenging the Gairy regime. He continued to forge ahead and to champion the causes of the downtrodden, defend them against injustice, end their exploitation, and to construct a new and just society.[10]

Between 1970 and 1979, although Bishop was many times the victim of searches, arrests, police brutality and imprisonment, he struggled unrelentingly for justice and equality, and refused to be outdone by Gairy's wit, parody, overt hostility, and violence. Throughout this period, he continued to actively engage himself in promoting the quality of life of both the working class peoples and the poor. His march forward was toward "national independence, economic liberation, development and social progress.[10] As Bishop put it, it was "Forward Ever, Backward Never."[11]

### 1970 and Beyond

The Black Power demonstration that we alluded to earlier, was not the only mass uprising that Gairy had to contend with during this time. In fact, it was only the beginning of a period of intense opposition to the Gairy regime. In early 1970, nurses at the St. George's General Hospital took to the streets to protest against the working conditions to which they were subjected, and to let the public know that medical supplies were acutely short and hygienic conditions most horrible. The nurses were joined in this protest by both a number of other working class groups and most of the nation's high school students who, by this time, were also beginning to scrutinize Gairy. Unwilling to tolerate mass demonstrations against his regime, Gairy struck back at the demonstrators by arresting dozens of them on charges ranging from conspiracy to mutiny. One of the persons arrested was Maurice Bishop. In the end, all of those arrested who were charged and later brought to trial were acquitted.

A series of protests and mass demonstrations followed this incident. In the period immediately following 1970, dozens of demonstrations involving workers from almost every working class sector of the nation's economy,[12] took place. The main theme running through all of them was that Gairy was no longer wanted and must be removed from political office.

Worker dissatisfaction with the protest against the Gairy regime provided leverage for mass organization. It also conditioned the emergence of new political organizations[9] on the Grenadian scene. Two of the more important ones that emerged during this period were the Joint Endeavour for Welfare, Education and Liberation (J.E.W.E.L.), and the Movement for Assemblies of the People (M.A.P.).[13] The J.E.W.E.L. movement came into being in early 1972. This organization was founded by the Grenadian economist Unison Whiteman in the rural parish of St. David. Later in that same year, M.A.P. was founded by two young attorneys, Maurice Bishop and Kenrick Radix. J.E.W.E.L. operated mostly in the rural areas, while M.A.P. worked in the urban areas.

On March 11, 1973, J.E.W.E.L. and M.A.P. merged to form the N.J.M. Both Maurice Bishop and Unison Whiteman were elected joint political leaders of the N.J.M. Subsequent to its formation in 1973, the N.J.M. began to be recognized as the political organization that would liberate the Grenadian masses from the intense repression they were experiencing at the hands of Gairy.

The N.J.M. functioned as an effective political organization. Other than organizing and rallying the public against the Gairy regime, it dueled with the latter on every imaginable front and refused to submit to Gairy's threats and overt violence against the organization. For example, when Jeremiah Richardson, a young supporter of the N.J.M. was allegedly shot by Gairy's police[9], the N.J.M protested and organized mass demonstrations which were responsible for closing down Pearls Airport for a few days.

In Grenada, the N.J.M. was beginning to take charge. This was evident from the fact that since its formation, popular support for the

N.J.M. and opposition to the Gairy regime began to crystallize. Around mid-1973, Gairy left Grenada for London. While away, the N.J.M. organized two massive demonstrations. The first involved over 10,000 people, about one tenth of Grenada's population. The second rally which was held some months later, involved just as many people. During this rally, the demonstrators or "People's Congress" as they called themselves, accused and subsequently convicted Gairy of a number of crimes which included incompetence, widespread corruption and brutality. The "Peoples Congress" also called on Gairy to resign or face a national strike beginning on November 18.

Gairy refused to resign. Determined to silence his opponents, he, on the eve of the proposed strike, arrested six of the N.J.M.'s leaders including Maurice Bishop and Unison Whiteman. Bishop and Whiteman were subsequently brutally beaten by Gairy's men in what came to be regarded as the "Bloody Sunday" incident.

While most of the N.J.M.'s leaders were in jail, a number of anti-Gairy groups came together and formed a coalition that called itself the "Committee of 22". This group included members of the Grenadian Chamber of Commerce (G.C.C.) the Grenadian Teachers Union (G.T.U.), Civil Service organizations, anti-Gairy Unions, churches, and many middle-class oriented groups from all over the country. According to the *Carib News* ". . .while this committee was in favour of reforms that would stabilize the society, it did not want any change in the capitalist system which the N.J.M. proposed." ₉ The "Committee of 22" wielded some power and influence during the absence of the N.J.M.'s leadership; it put forward proposals for an island-wide strike. It demanded that Gairy be held responsible. It also charged the police with the events of "Bloody Sunday ", and demanded that an end be put to the police state. After some initial resistance, Gairy finally agreed to the terms of the "Committee of 22" and the strike was subsequently called off.

But Gairy's promises were never kept. Although he did appoint a commission to investigate the "Bloody Sunday" incident, and listened to recommendations to disband the Mongoose Gang and make changes within the Police Service yet, in the end, he ignored these recommendations and, thus, reneged on his promises.

Realizing that Gairy had failed to keep his promise, both the "Committee of 22" and the N.J.M. leadership, now out of jail, proposed a nationwide strike beginning January 1, 1974. This strike, which lasted for three months, literally crippled the island.₉ During this period, there were "mass protests, police violence and popular reprisals against the police."₉ Perhaps the most unforgettable incident that occurred during this period was the killing on ' Bloody Monday' of Maurice Bishop's father, Rubert Bishop. Chris Searle in his book, *Grenada: The Struggle Against Destabilization,* describes this incident: "The climax came on 21 January when the Mongoose Gang and the Green Beast Troops, together with other Gairy hoodlums, stormed into Otway House, the headquarters of the Seamen and Waterfront Workers Union (S.W.W.U.) on the Carenage, or Inner Harbour, attacking demonstrators and finally killing Rupert Bishop, small businessman and father of Maurice, as he barred the doorway and protected a room full of women and schoolchildren."₁₄

Despite ongoing protests and much violence, Gairy managed to restore order to the country. He used a combination of methods to accomplish this. First of all, he received gifts and took loans from Britain, Canada, Guyana, Jamaica and Trinidad in an attempt to appease the appetite of the Grenadian workers. Second, he compromised with the "Committee of 22". Third, he overtly repressed the Grenadian citizenry. Fourth, he granted a few minor concessions.

**The New Jewel - A Populist Movement**

Despite Gairy's superficial committment to moderate means, the N.J.M. used every means at its disposal to paint Gairy as a strong-armed leader. The "Bloody Sunday" incident, in particular, appeared on television and radio programs in the Caribbean, London, and New York. Local newspapers called for the disbandment of the Mongoose Gang. The Duffus Commission of Inquiry report agreed with the local newspapers and called for the disbandment of the gang. The report further said:

1. The Police Aides

    From the evidence given and from available records it has been clearly established that the Police Aides, or by whatever name they are known, were an unlawfully constituted body of men. Many of these Police Aides were violent men with long criminal records. Without any training or discipline they were called into being ostensibly to assist the regular police force but, instead, from their inception and throughout the time of their existence inflicted unspeakable atrocities upon many of the citizens of Grenada, especially on members of the New Jewel Movement on Sunday, November 18 and Monday, November 19, 1973. The veritable reign of terror culminated in being responsible for a riot on the Carenage, St. George's on Monday, January 21, 1974, and the consequent death of Mr. Rupert Bishop.

The first specific recommendation therefore of this Commission is that the Police Aides should be completely disbanded and never again called into service.

During the course of this evidence the Honourable Prime Minister gave the Commissioners his solemn verbal assurance that the Police Aides would be completely disbanded. In this connection, however, the Commissioners seriously question the advisability or the necessity of the establishment of another auxiliary arm of the regular police force - a so-called "Field Force" - or "Defense Force", especially when it is known that former police aides are now members of this Defense Force.

2. Re-Organization of the Police Force

The Commissioners strongly recommend as urgently and absolutely necessary a thorough re-organization of the Royal Grenada Police Force. To achieve its primary purpose of the maintenance of law and order, the re-organization of the Police Force is urgently required. Moreover, the re-organization of the Police Force is seen as highly desirable if the discipline and morale of the Force, which has been sadly eroded and weakened by recent events and the unlawful system of police aides, is to be restored and maintained.

To help in achieveing these ends the Commissioners recommended:

(i) Recruitment

A programme of recruitment should be undertaken to enlist into the Police Force candidates of a higher standard of education that exhibited by many who gave evidence before the Commission, for constables as well as officers.

(ii) Training of Recruits

A proper programme of training for all recruits must be undertaken and since the State of Grenada at the present time lacks both the personnel and suitable facilities for such basic training, it is recommended that sister Caribbean countries such as Barbados,

Trinidad and Tobago, or Jamaica be asked to assist in providing such training.

(iii) Training of Officers

Since the morale and efficiency of the Police Force depend in no small measure upon the quality of its leadership, every effort must be made to provide high quality leadership. As a first step towards the achievement must be undertaken and those officers who manifest qualities of leadership and competence should be given opportunities for training overseas.

Incompetence should not be rewarded with promotion on the grounds of seniority in the service nor should ability to please and carry out the wishes of politicians be stepping stones to advancement. On the other hand, fear of incurring the disfavour of political leaders should not stand between an officer and the execution of his duties. In many instances senior police officers as well as constables who appeared as Witnesses before the Commission admitted to failure or neglect in carrying out their duties. It appears that the underlying reason for such inaction in some cases was intimidation by police aides or fear of reprisal by incurring political displeasure. Glaring examples of this were the many instances of the failure of senior officers to take any action whatsoever against policemen and police aides who used violence to or abused prisoners.

(iv) Appointment of the Commissioner of Police

The key to the re-organization of the Police Force and to strengthening and improving discipline and morale lies in its leadership, especially in providing a highly qualified, competent and experienced person of integrity as the Commissioner of Police. It was observed that the position of Commissioner of the Royal Grenada Police Force within recent years has been filled by a series of acting appointments. The efforts of the Government to find suitable persons to fill the post are recognized, but it is the firm conviction of the Commissioners that the Public Serivce Commission be requested to take the necessary steps to implement this recommendation forthwith.[15]

**The Decline of Gairy's Rule**

In 1951, Gairy was riding the crest of a political wave. He was, by far, one of the most powerful and influential Grenadian leaders. By 1974, Gairy's leadership was definitely in trouble. What exactly did Gairy do to lose his political support? Was the demise of his leadership due to personal weakness? What role did class, race, skin color, family name and geographical location play in Gairy's fall from power?

Throughout his tenure in office Gairy made little effort to extend and intensify his political base of support. He relied instead on his personal charm, flamboyant personality, and charismatic leadership. During his administration he made "no attempt to organize the urban workers, not even taking advantage of the opportunities created, for example, when the Seamen and Waterfront Workers' Union severed itself from its branch membership in the Grenada Workers' Union in 1953. He never recognized the potential power of the urban workers in St. George's. . ."[16]

Gairy's leadership style was based on the concept that he was the hero and was unwilling to share power with anyone else. Archibald Singham in his book entitled *The Hero and the Crowd in a Colonial Polity,* said that Gairy "had developed neither a coherent policy nor a group of leaders around him; there was no inner circle' in the party, any type of inner circle that did exist was heavily dependent on Gairy's personal support in maintaining their electoral strength. He was careful not to allow any of his supporters to develop strong and viable constituency organizations; instead he always tried to maintain direct personal contact with each such organization. . ."[16] Instead of organizational strength, Gairy depended on community meetings at which he was the main speaker. At one of those meetings which one of the authors attended, Gairy said that "Grenadians would vote for a 'crapoo' (frog) if I say so." Any party member who sought to develop a constituency of his own was thrown out of the party. L.C.J. Thomas, the representative from St. John and St. Mark, was expelled from the G.U.L.P. when he sought to develop an organization in St. John and St. Mark.

Migration of farmers, laborers, fishermen and factory workers to Trinidad and England contributed to a further decline in Gairy's power. In 1951-52 it was estimated that the Grenada Manual and Mental Workers Union (G.M.M.W.U.) had about 6,000 paid and 10,000 unpaid members. By 1958 the respective estimates were 4,500 and 6,000. By 1962 membership was estimated to have fallen to 3,000. It should also be pointed out that there was a tremendous growth of rival trade unions in Grenada. In 1952 there were 5 registered trade unions in Grenada. By 1957 this number had risen to 12. In 1960 there were 4 strikes with the G.M.M.W.U. being responsible for only one. The strength of Gairy and his union, the G.M.M.W.U., was not what it had been in 1951. The increase in the number of functional trade unions helped to undermine Gairy's position as the trade union leader of Grenada. He now had to compete with trade unions like the Seamen and Waterfront Workers Union (S.W.W.U.), the Commercial and Industrial Workers Union (C.I.W.U.) and the Allied and Technical Workers Unions (A.T.W.U.). It should be of interest to point out that none of these unions represented the interest of the working class.

A review of the data reveals that the "creation" of these trade unions had as a major purpose the destruction of Gairy's leadership. He was unable to integrate the G.M.M.W.U. with the growing urban unions. The urban trade unions, on the other hand, indicated no desire for closer affiliation with the peasantry. They were determined to maintain their privileged positions. In 1952 the Grenada Agriculturist Union (G.A.U.) was formed. This union was anti-Gairy and sought to mobilize opinion against him in the rural areas.

The growth of welfare sponsored by state and employer and by cooperatives sought to neutralize Gairy's strengths in politics and leadership in the rural areas. "These quasi-bureaucratic agencies attempted for the most part to inculcate middle class and 'modern'values in the rural areas, thus reducing the peasants' dependence on both the union and the political party... Among the youth, Gairy has lost some of his appeal with the advent of 4-H Clubs; by 1961 there were 36 active clubs with a membership of 1,000."[16] Gairy's challenge of the social, political and economic order in 1951 brought about decided improvements, but his success did not bring the social equality which he craved. Gairy was not forgiven for the embarrassment he caused the plantation owners and the bureaucrats, especially the administrator, James M. Lloyd. Neither the government officials nor the white and brown elites would play tennis or have tea with Gairy. He was told, on several occasions, that Grenada was run by the economic and colonial elites and not the political leader.

Gairy's unwillingness to compromise his leadership caused him problems. As Premier and later Prime Minister, he was determined to personally run the affairs of the country. The ruling elite, on the other hand, were determined to use every means at their disposal to embarrass Gairy and to "cut him down to size". The ruling elite used the law, the established bureaucratic structure, and threats of mass demonstrations to keep Gairy, the people's hero, in his place.

One could simply stop here and say that Gairy was an evil, irrational and wicked leader. Such a conclusion, we feel, fails to capture the changing political climate that Grenada experienced. The changes that we refer to began in 1972, the year the Jewel Movement was formed. We cannot examine the changes whichoccurred in Grenada without looking at the changes which took place in international politics during the late fifties, the sixties, and seventies. The youth of most of the underdeveloped countries were clammering for change. "Ghana's independence in 1957, the Cuban revolution in 1959, the war of liberation waged by Algeria against French Colonialism, the Vietamese struggle against U.S. aggression, the growing rebelliousness of the Black population in the United States, the unilateral declaration of independence by racist Rhodesia, the imperialist plot against Lumumba in the Congo, were some of the events that contributed to the post-war generation's political awakening.' ₁₇

Bishop and the N.J.M. continued their attack on Gairy. This time, a demonstration was staged against a British landowner. Lord Brownslow, owner of the LaSagesse estate, was accused of preventing Grenadians from using a nearby beach. A public trial was conducted and Lord Brownslow was found guilty of "trampling upon the rights of the people". The demonstrators tore down the barrier to the beach road. Leading the demonstrators were members of the N.J.M. headed by a young economist named Unison Whiteman.

How did the Prime Minister, Eric Matthew Gairy, handle these incidents? What did he do to restore his charismatic leadership? How did he deal with Maurice Bishop and the N.J.M.? The Prime Minister, in a May 3, 1970 radio broadcast, outlined how he planned to deal with the "Black Power" advocates. He said:

"I cannot close my ears to the ugly incidents alleged to have taken place recently... A stitch in time saves nine is indeed a wise maxim. My government will not stand by and allow individuals or groups to agitate or incite, to promulgate or to promote any racial disharmony in this peaceful 'isle of spice' - the Caribbean Garden of Eden... I say, those guilty of molestation of any form should be told, 'Good Morning' by the Cat-O-Nine as they start their prison term. Law and order will always reign supreme in this great little state of ours."[15]

To supplement the existing police force, Gairy said that "a large number of special Secret Police ranging from businessman to the man in the street was also    in formation [but] there will be no uniforms to betray the secrecy of these persons."[15]

Gairy told the Duffus Commission that the police aides or the Mongoose Gang were not recruited under the Police ordinance and therefore did not have the authority to arrest, or the authority to charge. In an answer to a question on how the police aides were recruited, Gairy said: "Any time there is a situation...where people are subversive and they want to take over Government by force we hold a meeting. I call the police officers together and we determine the need to assist the police and then a date is fixed. We put something over the air, the people come. I am there myself, and I would give whatever assistance possible and the people would be recruited by the police officers."[15] In his quest to maintain power and control, the civil rights of many Grenadians were violated. The police aides did, on several occasions, arrest individuals who had angered the Prime Mninster. The arrest of Eric Randall Campbell, a member of the N.J.M., by police aides Willie and Moslyn Bishop, Albert Clarke, Lennard Noel and Raphael Brizan tells the story:

> "Eric Randall Campbell of LaSagesse, St. Davids, is a maintenance engineer employed by Jonas, Brown and Hubbards, reputedly the largest firm in Grenada. Mr. Campbell is also a member of the New Jewel Movement. About 3 o'clock on Monday, November 19, 1973, he went to the St. David's Post Office and Revenue Office to collect mail. As he was about to descend the steps to leave he saw police aides Willie and Moslyn Bishop, Albert Clarke, Lennard Noel, and Raphael Brizan, (all members of the Mongoose Gang) ascending the steps. Brizan grabbed Campbell by the collar of his shirt and told him 'We are looking for you'. Campbell asked 'what for'? Brizan replied 'Don't ask me what for, the Premier say bring all you in dead or alive'. Together, the police aides took himself and Eslyn Christopher to the St. David's police station where Mosyln Bishop told P.C. Murray, who kept the diary, 'Hold this man here

for me and if you let him go your ass is going to pay for it'. Campbell and Christopher were consequently detained in the prisoners' section of the St. David's police station. Immediately after, Moslyn Bishop telephoned the Grenville police station and asked to speak to Assistant Superintendent Belmar and he was overheard to say 'We have Campbell and Christopher here, we are going in search of Teddy Grainger and Sam now'. Campbell and Christopher, who had been placed in a cell, were later taken in a motor car P 1504 driven by Raphael Brizan. Moslyn Bishop said they were being taken to St. George's. When the car reached Providence, Albert Clarke drove the car instead of Raphael Brizan who then went into the back seat and cuffed Campbell about the face and chest. Willie Bishop and Lennard Noel then pulled out revolvers. The car stopped at Vincennes where it was joined by a police vehicle driven by Sgt. Sayers with other police aides. Inquiries were made of Teddy Victor, the editor of the N.J.M.'s Newspaper. Victor was identified and the men ran after him but failed to catch him. In the meantime, a gun was fired by one of the men. The police party then left for Dudmar where Joseph Grainger was beaten with a baton by a police aide before the party set off again for St. George's where they were left in custody at the Central Police Station.''[15]

On November 4, 1973, the N.J.M. held a political meeting at Sea Moon and passed a resolution calling on Gairy and his government to resign on November 8, 1973. The text of The People's Indictment read as follows:

## THE PEOPLE'S INDICTMENT

*WHEREAS Government can only rule with the consent of the people*

*AND WHEREAS a Government is the servant (and not the master of the people and is under a moral duty to carry out the wishes of the people)*

*AND WHEREAS the people elect a Government to provide them with material benefits and to improve the quality of their lives*

*AND WHEREAS the PEOPLE expect to live free of fear, hunger, misery and expliotation*

*AND WHEREAS the PEOPLE have a sacred right to work in order to feed themselves, care for their families, educate themselves and their children, house and clothe themselves and obtain proper, adequate and cheap medical attention*

*AND WHEREAS the people are ALWAYS entitled to withdraw their consent and to remove a Government when it becomes clear that the Government is unable or unwilling to carry out their minimum wishes and supply them with their basic demands*

*AND WHEREAS the present Government of Grenada had demonstrated beyond any reasonable doubt both its unwillingness and its inability to carry out the wishes of the people, many of which were stated in the Manifesto issued by the party of the Government in the last elections.*

*AND WHEREAS conclusive proof of the inability and unwillingness of this Government to carry out its mandate to govern us according to our wishes and instructions is provided by the following MAJOR CRIMES committed by the Government against the people, to wit:*

*1. The Gairy Government encouraged and openly condoned the murders of our citizens: viz. Bro. Jerry Richardson, Bro. Cummings, Bro. Lester Richardson, and Bro. Allister Saunders, among others.*

*2. The Gairy Government ordered or condoned the shooting of the ten peaceful and unarmed demonstrators who were protesting the murder of Jerry Richardson by a member of the Police Force.*

*3. The Gairy Government has been carrying out its plan to rule the people by fear thus hiring known criminals to brutalize people who are bold enough to oppose its corrupt Government.*

*4. The Gairy Government has been using methods of malicious and arbitrary searches as a means of provoking and harassing opponents of its criminal Government in an attempt to stifle dissent.*

*5. The Gairy Government has squandered and continues to squander the people's money on dream projects employing political Civil Servants and squandering millions on unnecessary travel, arms and secret police while people are catching hell to make a living.*

*6. The Gairy Government has abused our laws in seizing the people's co-operatives. the Banana Co-operative and the Cocoa Association.*

*7. The Gairy Government confiscated the People Radio Station, and turned it into a propaganda machine for its personal satisfaction and glorification.*

45

8. *The Gairy Government has not accounted for the spending of the people's money in the G.M.M.W.U. from 1951 to today.*

9. *The Gairy Government must answer for the arbitrary dismissal of the brave and gallant nurses who protested against the appalling conditions which obtained at the General Hospital in 1970.*

10. *The Gairy Government has victimized hundreds of persons in the Police, Civil Service, Estates and among citizens generally since 1967 when it resumed office.*

11. *The Gairy Government has destroyed the Police Force, and turned it into a band of Legalized Criminals. It is Gairy who has sent known Criminals to associate with the Police, to spy on them, and commit acts to belittle and embarrass them.*

12. *The Gairy Government destroyed Agriculture in the State. It did so by the acquisition (through spite) of highly productive estates and cutting them up in the land for the landless scandal. It destroyed our Agricultural Stations, and Westerhall Farms bears testimony to this.*

13. *The Gairy Government has sold out all Government lands and buildings. Quarantine Station is gone. Even the Mental Hospital and Alms House Lands are up for sale.*

14. *The Gairy Government has destroyed our Hospitals, and has endangered our health and lives with poor medical facilities; doctors are now afraid to remain in Grenada. There are no resident doctors in Carriacou, St. David's and Gouyave.*

15. *The Gairy Government has acquired people's property in an effort to deprive political opponents of their livelihood.*

16. *The Gairy Governmnet has destroyed our roads. Our main roads are deplorable. Feeder roads can now be remembered.*

17. *The Gairy Government has refused to hold public inquiries into the wanton shooting of our citizens, and into other national disasters such as the sinking of the City of St. George, and into conditions in the Police Force, Civil Service and Prisons.*

18. *The Gairy Government has conspired with Brownslow and others to take away people's rights to LaSagesse and other beaches.*

19. *The Gairy Government has refused to pay its dues to the Secondary Schools and the Universities. It has insulted youth by*

*demonstrating that the Secret Police come before youth.*

*20. The Gairy Government has transformed our democracy into a ruthless one-man dictatorship. Gairy's dreams are our plans. The entire country is now run as his private estate.*

*21. The Gairy Government has enriched itself among other ways by taking salaries for the entire clique.*

*22. The Gairy Government has shown its complete contempt of and disregard for the people's wishes by its approach to the question of Independence.*

*23. The Gairy Government has done nothing to reduce the scandalously high cost of living and by its policy of raising taxes on the essential foods and other items like rice, flour and kerosene it has increased the level of poverty in the island.*

*24. The Gairy Government has increasingly been giving away our best lands to foreigners.*

*25. The Gairy Government was BORN IN BLOOD, BAPTIZED IN FIRE, CHRISTENED WITH BULLETS, IS MARRIED TO FOREIGNERS AND IS RESULTING IN DEATH TO THE PEOPLE.*

*26. The Gairy Government has made no effort to provide us with a sense of direction and a worthwhile sense of purpose.*

*27. The Gairy Government has consistently neglected throughout its years in office from 1951 onwards the basic needs of the people for decent housing, adequate clothing, reliable transport, cheap and high quality medical facilities, a better quality of education for all our children, the development (instead of destruction) of our Agriculture for us to feed all our people and the denial of the opportunity to work and earn a livelihood of over half of the people. These are the gravest crimes of which a Government can stand accused and be proved guilty.*

*AND WHEREAS the PEOPLE of Grenada have now decided that for the reasons given above we must decide on the best course of action now open to us to save Grenada.*

*NOW THEREFORE BE IT RESOLVED that a Congress of the People Meeting at Sea Moon on the 4th day of November 1973 had democratically and collectively agreed to take the following actions:*

*(a) To pass a verdict of guilty on the charges laid against*

*this Government and to condemn this Government for irresponsibility, corruption, incompetence, inefficiency, breach of contract, and to pass a vote of no confidence in the Government.*

*(b) To call upon this Government to resign with effect from 18th November, 1973.*

*(c) To appoint a National Unity Council from among persons present at this Congress charged with the responsibility of implementing the decision taken at the Congress to remove this Government from office and to constitute a provisional Government of the People pending the call of New Elections by the Governor to elect a new Popular Government.*

*(d) To agree to use the New Jewel Movement's manifesto for power to the People as the basis of a new plan that the new Government will operate to run the country.*

*AND BE IT FURTHER RESOLVED THAT COPIES OF THIS Resolution of the PEOPLE'S WILL be forwarded to the Governor, Premier and Cabinet as official notice of our decisions taken today.*[15]

The evidence of what was to be done in the event the government did not resign appeared in the November 9, 1973, issue of The New Jewel. Part of the plan called for the complete shutdown of the island. This meant that the people would "refuse to work, refuse to pay taxes, come out in the street in tens of thousands, inform the world of our struggle.. " [15] The information further stated that after Gairy's government is removed from power the Unity Council will consult with the trade unions, people and workers of Grenada as to the timing for new elections to choose a new government. Bishop said repeatedly that the aim of the N.J.M. is to seize political power from the hands of the government and place that power in the hands of the people. He insisted that this must be achieved "by any means necessary".

The demands of the N.J.M. were accompanied with direct actions. During this period, the N.J.M. held several meetings. At these meetings they criticized the system of government, the independence plans, the police, and preached violent methods of overthrowing Gairy's government. The purpose of the People's National Congress which was held at Sea Moon on November 4 was to decide ways and means of transferring political power to the members of the N.J.M.

Article 88 section 9 of the Duffus Commission of Inquiry report states that "stepped-up activities by the N.J.M., the preaching of violence and threats to government have clearly indicated subversion within the movement."[15] (1) Were the members of the N.J.M. serious about the takeover of the state? (2) Was Gairy simply using the stepped-up activities of the N.J.M. as an excuse to justify his violent and repressive actions. The Duffus Commission Report is correct when it says that "the documentary evidence supports the view that the N.J.M. was vigorously campaigning for a change of government."[15] The members constantly condemned Gairy's leadership and pursuaded Grenadians to rise up against the evils of the G.U.L.P.

Gairy was determined to overcome the criticisms and threats of the N.J.M. He was also profoundly committed to political independence. This commitment to achieving political independence by February, 1974, led him to claim that any opposition to his government, or to his government's plan, had to be vigorously crushed. The Duffus Commission of Inquiry report found that Gairy was "inspired by the high purpose of political independence. . . and became convinced that the activity of the N.J.M. was subversive to the State of Grenada."[15] Gairy accused the N.J.M. of stealing 50 rifles from the armory at Presentation College.

The reports received by Gairy from his security advisors told him that the N.J.M. posed a direct threat to the security of Grenada. The assessment of the Special Branch of the Police Force on November 12 stated that "the current increased activities of the N.J.M., the daily campaigning and threats to take over Government pose a direct threat to the security of the state."[15] As head of state and Minister of National Security, Gairy was prepared to take whatever steps necessary to ensure that the members of the N.J.M. did not have their way of preventing the independence which was scheduled for February, 1974.

The members of the N.J.M., on the other hand, were determined to overthrow Gairy's government. The N.J.M. had always made it clear that its aims were to do away with the electoral system and replace it with a system of Assemblies. In an interview with Alister Hughes and John Redman, Bishop outlined the objectives of the N.J.M. as follows: "The New Jewel Movement was an unconventional type of organization: it wasn't formed as an electoral political party but was formed as a political party that was more aimed at raising consciousness and with the declared intention of taking political power in or out of elections if the accepted processes did not allow for electoral change."[18] Bishop further said that the people of Grenada have a right to remove an oppressive government that did not respond to the needs of the people. In addition, he viewed Westminister democracy as equally oppressive because, as he put it, it does not come from the grass roots.

## Gairy Responds to the New Jewel Movement

Before we conclude this chapter, it might be helpful to examine the type of leadership that develops in colonial or former colonial societies like Grenada. In this setting the political leader must have strong support from the masses, from whom he demands total and complete loyalty. Any deviation from this is viewed as a direct threat to the colonial leader's ability to govern. Gairy, after the 1951 uprising, was forced to routinize his rule. He surrounded himself with loyal civil servants, a loyal police force, and the Mongoose Gang who were determined, at any cost, to protect and uphold their hero. This person's rise to power is based on the fact that he is willing to sacrifice his career for the well-being of the masses. Maurice Bishop, a constitutional lawyer, and a member of the upper middle class, "sacrificed" his career in order to struggle for food, jobs, and justice for the working class. This leader stresses constitutional advancement. On the other hand, there is the hero who comes from humble origins and bases his claim to political leadership on his role as a trade union leader. This leader, as in the case of Gairy, draws the largest of his support from the rural estate workers, the fisherman, the store clerks and the unemployed. He is sometimes viewed by his admirers and supporters as a person sent by God to ease their sufferings. Eric Gairy falls into this category. In spite of the class differences and leadership styles of Gairy and Bishop, they shared certain similarities. Archibald Singham, said that both types of leadership "tend to develop personal organization which are essentially authoritarian."[19]

Both Gairy and Bishop knew that in societies that are both colonial and agrarian, the leader must possess a certain tint of charisma. This special kind of charisma is "capable of mobilizing the crowd, but not developing a sustained mass following."[19] Unlike his brother in Africa, the West Indian colonial leader has no traditional culture to escape into. "One consequence of this type of political value system that differentiates between rational and irrational demands for change. . . The object of his rebelliousness is not clearly focused: the individual is against the state, or the economic conditions he suffers under, or just against 'them'. Electoral politicians, and particularly the hero, exploits this hostility and provides temporary relief for the masses through crowd Catharsis."[19]

The aims of these leaders are not to politicize meaningfully the masses, but instead to offer temporary solutions of problems which the hero has no real control over. Accordingly, a high premium is placed on the personal charisma of the leader. The ability to control the masses lies in the fact that the hero can get things done. In other words, he is seen as one who has a direct line to the power elite. In order to counter the appeal of the hero, the middle class elite must either come up with a hero of their own or mobilize opinion against the mass hero by themselves adopting the strategy of the crowd. The middle class party does this by substituting demagogic appeals for ideology.

The struggle for political power between Bishop and Gairy is a case in point. As mentioned earlier, Gairy had the support of the lower classes especially those in the rural areas. Bishop knew of this support and, therefore, decided that one way of weakening Gairy's power was to depict him as an evil man. According to Chris Searle, whenever Gairy did anything "the 'Jewel' were there to expose him, to organize his violence and fraudulence and pour scorn upon his obscurantism and 'ufology'."[20] This approach proved to be very successful. The unofficial opposition provided by the N.J.M. called on Gairy to resign, and to provide better health, housing, and employment facilities. The former knew that some of its requests were unattainable. Requests were made to embarrass the government and to generate public sympathy. The N.J.M.'s plans, on every occasion, accomplished its goals and objectives.

The N.J.M. held several public meetings at which they organized and educated the youth, the unemployed and the workers. The Jewel, the party's newspaper, criticized Gairy. These criticisms, needless to say, led to confrontation with the Prime Minister. A supporter of the N.J.M. told us that "they were prepared to take whatever steps necessary to remove the dictator from office. We knew that we had him up against the wall and that eventually he would have to strike out at us. . . We also knew that some of our supporters would be beaten, jailed and even killed. Our meetings, demonstrations, threats, rhetoric, and confrontations were designed to aggravate Gairy and therefore force him to retaliate. Whenever he retaliated, we used the incident to champion our cause. At one point Gairy was really confused. He did not fully understand our methods and consequently resorted to fighting fire with fire. This was his biggest mistake."[21] When we asked Mr. S.S. to explain Gairy's biggest mistake he told us that Grenadians do not condone violence and saw acts of violence against the Jewel as cruel and barbaric. He further told us that the N.J.M.'s plan to destroy Gairy's leadership was accomplished well before the 1974 independence.

Mr. S.S. might be correct when he said that Gairy did not know how to deal with the N.J.M.'s opposition. For one thing, he took the insults of the N.J.M. personally and simply "fought fire with fire". In his many radio broadcasts he labeled them as socialists, communists, and misfits. The N.J.M. were masters in the art of political provocation and the more Gairy attacked them the more they resorted to calling him names. They referred to him as the "obeah man", "master of U.F.O.'s", "the puppet" and the "deposed leader". It soon became "a war of words, a war of nerves, between Gairy and the N.J.M. with both parties claiming the support of the 'vast majority' of the people, and Gairy having at his disposal the 'forces and law and order'. . . and the Jewel claiming to have the moral authority of the people".[21]

The N.J.M.'s art at political organization and political agitation kept Gairy on the defensive. They blamed Gairy for everything that happened in Grenada. For example, the N.J.M. staged demonstrations and demanded the arrest of a member of the Royal Grenada Police Force (R.G.P.F.) when Jeremiah Richardson was murdered in Grenville, St. Andrew's. The N.J.M. was able to secure for the parents of Jeremiah Richardson a conviction against the policeman responsible for their son's death. These dramatic demands caught the attention of the local, and international news media. Gairy was depicted in the local and international media as a mystic and a U.F.O. freak. According to Sam Manuel and Andrew Pulley, "Gairy was also a mystic. He has given speeches at international forums on U.F.O.'s. He even made governmental decisions based on his dreams. . . there is a story about how he had a dream about circles. The next day he ordered that traffic circles be built all over the island. You come across these circles even in remote areas of the country."[22]

So for the first time the charisma of the hero was being questioned by some of his most loyal supporters. Gairy tried to regain his power and respectability by resorting to physical force and threats. His use of the Mongoose Gang and the Secret Police was ineffective in his efforts to restore order. Grenadians, even supporters of Gairy, came to view the members of the Mongoose Gang as criminals and therefore unfit to enforce law and order. By the end of 1974, for all practical purposes, Gairy's ability to lead Grenada was severely limited. He had lost his ability to politicize and mobilize the masses. He was unable to involve them in the decision-making process and in the formulation and implementation of policy. The commitment of most of his supporters became superficial. Many of them openly questioned Gairy's ability to govern the country. Some even suggested that Gairy, because of his evil deeds, had offended God and the N.J.M.'s opposition was therefore a sign. One of Gairy's loyal supporters told the authors just before the 1974 independence ceremonies that "Uncle Gairy should listen to God and resign before the election. . . he has always been a good man but apparently in recent times he has offended the Lord."[23]

## Tactics Used By The N.J.M.

The N.J.M.'s opposition of Gairy was well planned, well timed, expertly executed and forceful. Their main objective was to intimidate their opposition and to portray Gairy as an unfit leader. By March 13, 1979, the N.J.M. had achieved both objectives. How were these objectives achieved?

The N.J.M. attacked Gairy on several fronts. First of all, they portrayed him as a man who had outlived his usefulness. In an interview which took place in Cuba, Maurice Bishop and Unison Whitemanmade the following comments about the Prime Minister and the G.U.L.P. They said that despite the progressive beginnings "Gairy and his party turned into representatives of, and in part, members of the country's commercial bourgeoisie, closely tied to the interests of the big imperialist companies that exploit the island."[17] This statement is intended to show that Gairy and his party abandoned their mission of being representatives of the poor, the oppressed and the disenfranchised.

The next aim of the N.J.M. was to show that Gairy had become an oppressive leader. The former was out to demonstrate to the Grenadian public that the Prime Minister had abandoned the principles that he fought for in 1951. It accused Gairy of rigging the 1975 elections in an attempt to perpetuate his own political position and undermine that of his opponents. One might simply say that these accusations are meaningless since they are made every time elections are held. In the case of Grenada, these accusations had serious consequences for Gairy. Gairy's leadership was based on "hero worship". Because of this, the hero must be "a godly man", a person free from the blemishes of the sinful man. The N.J.M.'s questioning of Gairy's honesty created doubt in the minds of many of his supporters. No longer could Gairy accuse the administrator, a representative of the colonial power, of trying to frame him since this time he was accused by Grenadians.

Gairy was unable to mobilize and control the responses of the crowd as he did in 1951. "The mobilization of the crowd ultimately depends on the hero, who must be able to provide some form of political release, which Canetti terms the discharge, which temporarily relieves the anxiety of the crowd. The anxiety of the colonial man is of a neurotic kind which often incapacitates him from identifying with or participating in associations in the society on a rational basis. Neurotic anxiety makes it easy for him to identify with a hero, and this identification provides his political and often his social sense of belonging. However, instead of liberating the individual, this leads to further regression, making it more difficult to introduce rationality into political life."[19] As we already noted, between 1970 and 1979, Bishop had replaced Gairy as the leader of the crowd. Maurice Bishop, with his charismatic abilities and organizational skills, was able to provide the political release and discharge that we referred to above.

Gairy was also accused of forming alliances with dictatorial and oppressive governments. Both Bishop and Whiteman said that the "G.U.L.P. government is continuing its repressive policy and this year it has sought out international support and aid. Prime Minister Gairy visited Santiago, Chile, and a Chilean Lieutenant Colonel named Garcia Zamorano, who is very close to Pinochet himself, was in the island. As a result of these contacts, the Chilean fascist Junta is training and equipping Grenada's police and army."[17] Gairy was further accused of giving unlimited fishing rights in Grenada's waters to Chile and of developing ties with the Mafia. John Clancy whose real name is Eugene Zeck and who fled the United States, according to Bishop, was given a monopoly over the lobster and yachting industries. These accusations accomplished their objectives. They alluded to the fact that Gairy had lost touch with the masses and therefore had to resort to force and "underhanded" dealing with oppressive governments in order to maintain social order in Grenada.

The members of the N.J.M. were not about to stop their attacks. They said that Gairy did very little to reduce unemployment or better the working conditions of the laborers. They said that over 55 percent of the population were unemployed. They further noted that "the imperialist sectors control our financial institutions as well as the insurance companies. All the large hotels are in imperialist hands, and the public services - electricity, telephone - are as well. . ."[17]

Bishop explained that the N.J.M.'s main goal was to organize the working class, the youth, women, the middle class, and the farmers. The N.J.M.'s levels of organization were grass roots in nature. They held daily meetings with farmers, fishermen, factory workers, the poor and the displaced. Their rhetoric offered Grenadians hope and a longing for a new beginning. Careful examinations of the N.J.M.'s manifesto quickly point out their unwillingness to work within the framework of the Westminister model. The Westminister Model is a democratic form of government patterned after the British system. This is the system of government that existed in Grenada prior to the March 13, 1979 revolution. Instead, Bishop talked about a socialist option for Grenada. "The victory of socialism in our country will be possible only through firm ties with the socialist world and with the close cooperation of the most advanced governments of the region." [17]

" Socialism is the future we would like to see in Grenada. At present the reality is that the most backward forms of capitalist exploitation exists in Grenada. . . We know how poor and backward our country is. And we know how difficult it would be to resist the general economic and political pressures that imperialism would unleash against Grenada if it tried to break the bonds of domination. . .However, despite all the difficulties, we feel that the perspectives for the cause of social revolution in Grenada are good."[17]

Most of the data that we looked at in conducting this study pointed to the fact that the N.J.M.'s political agenda was much larger than the removal of Gairy from political office. Instead, the N.J.M. wanted to build a "just and free society" patterned along the Marxist/Lennist path. The mass demonstrations, people's congress, and political rhetoric used against Gairy were strategies used by the N.J.M. to legitimize their movement and claim to political power. Bishop knew that many Grenadians were not educated or curious enough to examine critically the N.J.M.'s manifesto and the direction that the new party offered Grenada. Grenadians were caught up in the rhetoric and charismatic leadership of Maurice Bishop. He was followed because he offered Grenadians, especially the poor and the young, an opportunity "to control their own destiny." His followers saw him as a leader who was "endowed with supernatural, superhuman, or at least specifically exceptional powers or qualities."[24] He used this "gift" of charisma to attempt to change attitudes, values, norms and patterns of behavior of Grenadians. In other words, he used his charisma as a revolutionary force.

Like Gairy, Bishop's charismatic leadership had to be managed and maintained since it was "born out of suffering, conflicts and enthusiasm."[24] Unlike Gairy, Bishop had to prove to both his supporters and foes that his Marxist/Lennist approach was the answer to Grenada's social, political and economical problems. As a charismatic leader, he had to find ways to legitimize his rule. He accomplished his objectives by pointing to the evils of the Gairy administration. The N.J.M. knew that deviance and respectability are necessarily linked. By pointing to the "deviant" nature of Gairy's administration, the N.J.M., at the same time, highlighted their respectability. Jack D. Douglas is correct when he said that: *the more intense the belief in good, or the striving for it, the more intense will be the belief in evil, or the attacks on good. An age of saints, will also necessarily be an age of satans or demons, and vice versa. An individual striving for goodness will to the same degree be striving against evil, and vice versa.*[25]

"An individual who is seen as not acting in accord with the absolute morality or, even more, one seen to be challenging the absolute majority and, therefore, threatening the foundations of social order - becomes subject both to condemnation by any segment of the public that wants to attack him (for whatever reason) and, more importantly, to (public) stigmatization by official control agents. We have a situation, then, in which any challenge to the absolute morality can lead to official stigmatization, including arrests and imprisonment. . . regardless of the amount of private support one might actually have among the general public. . ."[25]

The N.J.M. portrayal of Gairy assisted Grenadians in constructing a definition of the situation. Their portrayal of the Prime Minister as crazy, power hungry, an advocate of U.F.O.'s and the leader of the Mongoose Gang were sufficient to cause Grenadians to question his authority. Peter Berger was correct when he said that man constructs activities and patterns of actions as he attracts meanings to his everyday existence.[26] Social reality is thus both a conceptual reality and phenomenal reality. Having constructed several social realities, many Grenadians held on to them. The role of the N.J.M. was simply to keep Gairy on the defensive and to portray him as a shepherd who had lost his sheep. The N.J.M. continued its personal attacks on Gairy and, "became the vanguard of the revolution and it devolved upon that organization to devise the specific strategy and tactics for the liberation of the people."[27]

On March 12, 1979 Gairy took a trip to New York. "He left orders to murder Maurice Bishop and other leaders of the New Jewel Movement. The N.J.M. got wind of his plot and decided to act immediately. At 4:15 in the morning, about forty people destroyed the army base at True Blue."[2] "Next, the radio station was seized and the news of the revolution broadcast to the nation."[27] Writes Richard Jacobs, "Gairy's method of operation was so centralized and personalized that even the Mongoose Gang had to await specific instructions from Gairy before they were able to take any action. When the leaders of this criminal element were captured by the P.R.A. at about 7:00 a.m. on the morning of March 13, they were in the midst of a telephone conversation with Gairy."[27] Later that day, most cabinet members surrendered: a couple managed to escape by boat. By the early morning hours the following day, police stations were also taken over and brought under the hegemony of the N.J.M. "Only two people who resisted the revolutionary forces. . . were shot. One other person was accidentally killed. And so within twelve hours, with three people dead, the Grenada revolution had been accomplished."[27] The N.J.M. had decisively overthrown the politically corrupt regime of Eric Gairy, and had now come to take political power.

# CHAPTER THREE

# THE GRENADA REVOLUTION

# AND

# AFTERMATH: A CHRONOLOGY

## Introduction

This chapter will present a chronological account of the Grenada revolution and its aftermath. However, the aim is not simply to state the dates and facts of what actually happened during this period but, also, to indicate and highlight those events that culminated in the failure of the revolution.

The analysis of the Grenada revolution and its aftermath will be viewed in terms of four specific time-frames. The first time-frame began on March 13, 1979, and extended to October 13, 1983, a period of roughly four and one-half years. During this period the government of Eric Matthew Gairy was overthrown by the N.J.M. led by Maurice Bishop, a British-educated lawyer and a popular political figure who became the new Prime Minister. He assured Grenadians that the revolution was for food, for justice, and for democracy. Immediately after the take over of March 13, Bishop promised to hold "open and free" elections as soon as a new constitution could be written. In his first speech he assured the people of Grenada that all democratic freedoms including freedom of elections, religion and political opinion would be fully restored.

But, the Prime Minister quickly reneged on his promises. Rather than fulfill the expectations and aspirations of the Grenadian masses, as promised, Bishop proceeded to pursue secretly a course of action that emphasized a huge military buildup, and one that was purposely designed to misrepresent the true aims of the revolution to the local citizenry. By 1983, Bishop had allegedly become an unpopular leader; his leadership was questioned by the Central Committee of the N.J.M. which accused him of lacking both ideological clarity and the ability to move the party forward along Leninist lines of organization and discipline. On October 13, 1983, he was placed under house arrest by a rival faction of the N.J.M. which included many members of the Central Committee. This faction was headed by Bishop's own deputy, Bernard Coard, who was involved in a process of political dueling with Bishop to assume supreme control of the N.J.M.

The second period began on October 14, 1983, and terminated on October 23, 1983. During this period political dissention within the ranks of Prime Minister Maurice Bishop's regime began escalating. In fact, it was precisely such dissention that led to the resignation of the Deputy Prime Minister, and exacerbated the long standing political split between the two rival factions of the N.J.M. More importantly, the arrest and subsequent execution of the Prime Minister, as well as the military coup that followed, were the main events of this period. The increasing concern over this situation and its implications for the Caribbean region coupled with the possibility of an alleged United States invasion of the island were also issues to contend with.

The third phase of the Grenada Revolution began on October 24, 1983, and ended on October 30, 1983. This period was initially marked with a joint buildup of United States and Caribbean troops - troops that were later used to invade Grenada. However, the most significant event of this period was the military invasion of this tiny Caribbean island and the bloody overthrow of both the ruling military junta and leftist dissidents by invading U.S. forces. Also characteristic of this period was a short-lived popularity enjoyed by the Reagan administration, but one that was soon destroyed by criticisms from the international community as well as from individuals, groups and organizations within the geographical and ecological confines of the United States itself. The analysis of this period winds down with the return of a state of normalcy to Grenada and indications of the beginning of the evacuation of United States military forces from the island.

The fourth and final period begins on October 31, 1983, and extends to the present. During this period, repercussions of the Grenada invasion continued to haunt the Reagan administration. More importantly, this period was essentially a time of the rebuilding of Grenada. A number of things were important here: (1) the appointment of an interim government for the island; (2) the ridding of socialist elements from the society, and; (3) the reinstitution of a capitalist mode of production. This period also witnessed a reaffirmation by the United States to provide military socio-economic, and political aid to the island in its long road to recovery. The period culminated with Grenada holding general elections on December 3, 1984.

A Chronology of the Grenada Revolution and its Aftermath.
Time-Frame One: March 13, 1979 to October 13, 1983.

The revolution of March 13, 1979, changed the political, economical and social structure of Grenada. In this section we will trace the events that led to these changes.

On the morning of March 13, 1979, Maurice Bishop, in his first radio broadcast to the residents of Grenada said: "We have taken over the Government and the country. We were tired and fed up of running, of being brutalized by the Secret Police. We were tired of seeing our brothers and sisters suffer in too many ways. The government was economically and politically bankrupt. We saw a definite moral decline and we could not let our country get into complete moral bankruptcy also. In addition, when we established very definitely the plans to wipe out the leaders of the N.J.M. on the night of March 12, 1979, we knew that the time had come for us to act. So we took the collective decision to strike, it was them or us."[1]

The revolution took everyone, except those who planned and executed it, by surprise. It was, nevertheless, welcomed by Grenadians at home and abroad. Many Grenadians saw the N.J.M. and the charismatic leadership of Maurice Bishop as a welcomed alternative to the tyrannical rule of Eric Gairy. Bishop, in his first radio address, promised that the revolution would benefit everyone, regardless of political opinion, or which political party one supported. He also emphasized the need to build a democratic revolution. As he put it, "With the working people we made our popular, anti-imperialist, and democratic revolution. . . with them we will build and advance to socialism and final victory."[2]

Bishop and the N.J.M. were determined not to repeat the mistakes that Gairy made. They said that "Gairy fell victim to the same colonial conditioning as did the people against whom he was fighting in the initial stages of his struggle so that he was unable to bring his struggle to its logical conclusion--the transformation of Grenada into a country of greater opportunities for all and a more equitable society where greater freedoms and true democracy would be the guiding principles upon which the society would depend."[1] Maurice stressed that it was for this reason that the people rebelled on March 13. In his interview with D. Sinclair Dabreo, Bishop pointed out that his untrained comrades were driven by the desire to restore democracy to Grenada. He further pointed out that there were Cubans in Grenada on the day of the revolution: it is alleged that Cuban Commandos actually helped to organize the revolution and take over the army barracks at True Blue. Bishop knew that the revolution would not succeed without strong military support from the P.R.A. He sought to consolidate his position by strengthening the armed forces. The following data released by the United States Department of State and Department of Defense, and here reported verbatim, attests to this.

## The Military Buildup

When the N.J.M. took power in 1979, Grenada had a British-style constabulary and a small and lightly-armed defense force. By October 25, 1983, Grenada had a regular army approaching 600, supplemented by a militia estimated at between 2,500 and 2,800 members.

The decision to create a state militia was announced soon after Bishop took power. The militia's mission was to assist the army in national defense, to perform neighborhood control duties, and to serve as a vehicle for ideological recruitment and indoctrination. Militia members were uniformed but unsalaried, and received two months of basic infantry training at army camps or other sites, followed by two-hour classes each week largely devoted to political education. Service in the militia gradually came to be seen as a prerequisite for government employment.

In January, 1981, the P.R.G. formed the People's Revolutionary Armed Forces (P.R.A.F.), composed of the P.R.A., the People's Revolutionary Militia (P.R.M.), the Grenada Police Service (G.P.S.), the Coast Guard, the Prison Service, the Fire Service, and the Cadet Corps. General Hudson Austin, a former prison guard, was placed in command of both the P.R.A.F. and the P.R.A.

Although its forces already dwarfed those of its Organization of Eastern Caribbean States (O.E.C.S.) Grenada was planning to field three more active battalions and nine more battalions in reserve. A July 2, 1982, request by the P.R.A.F. to the Armed Forces of the Soviet Union (A.F.S.U.) reads as follows:

The plan for the development of the Armed Forces during the three (3) year period 1983 to 1985 for which the assistance is required is as follows:

1983 - (i) Further consolidation of:

(a) One Permanent Infantry Battalion.

(b) Five (5) Reservist Infantry Battalions plus assurance and support units.

(ii) The creation of:

(a) Two (2) more regular Infantry Battalions.

(b) Four (4) more reservist Battalions plus assurance and support units.

1984 - Formation of one additional regular Infantry Battalion together with two (2) reservist battalions plus assurance and support units.

1985 - Formation of three (3) additional reservist battalions plus assurance and support units.

The proposed 18-battalion force, even if organized into relatively small battalions along Cuban lines, would put 7,200 men and women under arms. Battalions of more conventional size would raise this to some 10,000 or more, excluding personnel on the general staff and in other support functions. In proportion to population, this would have given Grenada one of the largest military forces of any country in the world.

### Military Agreements With the Soviet Union, Cuba, and North Korea

Documents found by the U.S.-Caribbean security forces on the island indicate that in the last three years, Grenada signed at least five military assistance agreements: Three with the Soviet Union, one with Cuba and one with North Korea. The existence of a similar agreement with Czechoslovakia is suggested by a bill of lading and by an extensive memorandum written in the Grenadian embassy in Havana, which also mentions a military agreement with Bulgaria.

**Secrecy.** All of Grenada's military agreements were secret. The agreements with the U.S.S.R. commit both governments to taking "all necessary measures to ensure keeping in secret the terms and conditions of the deliveries, all the correspondence and information connected with (their) implementation." The protocol with Cuba provides that Grenada and Cuba will "assure the secrecy of the permanency of the military personnel in both states and the character of the activities, as well as the mail and information related to the present Protocol."

**What was to be provided.** Taken together, the Soviet, Cuban, North Korean and inferred Czechoslovakian agreements provide for delivery by 1986 of the following (excludes some small weapons and support items):

— About 10,000 assault and other rifles, including Soviet AK-47's, Czech M-52/57's, sniper rifles and carbines;

— More than 4,500 submachine and machine guns;

— More than 11.5 million rounds of 7.62mm ammunition;

— 294 portable rocket launchers with more than 16,000 rockets;

— 85 - 82mm mortars with more than 4,800 mortar shells;

— 12 - 75mm cannon with some 600 cannon shells;

— 60 crew-served anti-aircraft guns of various sizes, with almost 600,000 rounds of ammunition;

— 86 other vehicles and earthmovers;

— 4 costal patrol boats;

— 156 radio stations;

— More than 20,000 sets of uniforms; and

— Tents capable of sheltering more than 5, 000 persons.

This listing includes enough to outfit a force of 10,000 with half that number in the field.

## The Cuban Role

**Early arms deliveries.** Cuba began to provide arms as soon as the N.J.M. seized power. A 1981 memo from the Grenadian Chief of Staff lists the following weapons received from Cuba in April 1979.
— 3,400 Soviet and U.S. rifles with 3 million rounds of ammunition;
— 200 machine-guns with a half-million rounds of ammunition;
— 100 pistols with 66,000 rounds;
— 100 shoulder-fired rocket launchers with 4,000 rockets;
— 12 - 82 mm mortars with 4,800 mortar shells;
— 12 - 75 mm cannon with 600 shells; and
— 12 - 12.7 mm anti-aircraft guns with 237,000 rounds.

These 3,800 infantry weapons and 36 artillery pieces arrived in Grenada long before the government had begun to organize its expanded military establishment.
Cuba's rapid response is a good measure of its early interest in Grenada.

**Cuba as Soviet intermediary.** Cuba also took the lead in developing the Soviet block's military relationship with Grenada. The first two Soviet agreements were signed in Havana. The terms of all of the agreements with the U.S.S.R. called for Soviet delivery of arms and supplies to Cuba for transshipment to Grenada. When in 1981, Prime Minister Bishop wished to send Army General Hudson Austin to the Soviet Union to discuss additional needs and assistance, he wrote to "Comrade Raul" (probably Raul Castro) asking for "advice and suggestions on the best ways to present this document to the Soviets." It was through the Grenadian embassy in Havana that Grenada formally requested the meeting with the Soviets. A bill of lading for "1,250 cases of explosive ammunition (warheads, rockets)" sent by Czechoslovakia shows that other supplies followed the Soviet pattern of shipping via Cuba.

**Military Training.** A signed but undated treaty with Cuba provided for nine Cuban military "specialists" to be stationed permanently in the General Staff of the P.R.A. and twenty to be stationed in the field with Grenadian units. In addition, more Cuban military personnel were to be assigned temporarily, six to the General Staff and six or seven elsewhere in Grenada. Their mission was to "assist Grenadian military men on the questions of Organization of the Organic Structure, Organization of the Instruction and combative and campaign training of the troops and staffs... and in the laboration of the operative and mobilization plans for the defense of the country." Teams of experts were to be made available for service in Grenada, and scholarships were to be provided to train Grenadians in Cuban military centers.

## The Soviet Role

**Arms deliveries.** The three Soviet agreements cited in this report provide for delivery between 1980 and 1986 of more than 1,000 pistols, more than 4,000 submachine guns, more than 90 portable rocket launchers, 7,000 land mines, 15,000 hand grenades and virtually all of Grenada's heavier artillery and heavier ammunition: 84 mortars, 400 heavy machine-guns, 48 anti-aircraft guns, 50 GRAD-P howitzers, 30 field guns, and 30 anti-tank guns. The agreements also furnish sixty armored personnel carriers and patrol vehicles, in addition to 86 other military-related vehicles, and some 14,000 uniforms.

**Military Training.** According to captured documents, the Union of Soviet Socialist Republic (U.S.S.R.) also provided specialist training and courses for selected high ranking officers. Army Chief of Staff Einstein Louison attended a six-month course in the Soviet Union. Both of Grenada's two Deputy Secretaries of Defense, Lt. Col. Liam James and Lt. Col. Ewart Layne, went to the U.S.S.R. for training. All three Soviet-Grenadian military agreements called for sending Grenadian servicemen to the U.S.S.R. for training. All three Soviet-Grenadian military agreements called for sending Grenadian servicemen to the U.S.S.R. to be trained in the use of the promised Soviet equipment. The treaty signed in July, 1982, also stipulated that Soviet specialists would be sent to Grenada.

**Intelligence Training.** In addition to military training, the Soviet Union also furnished intelligence and security training for a handful of Grenadians. A letter dated February 17, 1982, from Army Commander Hudson Austin to the then chairman of the K.G.B., Yuri Andropov, requested training for three Grenadians for one year in counter-intelligence and one Grenadian in intelligence.

**Use of Economic "Cover".** The United States (U.S.)-Caribbean security forces found Soviet weaponry in crates marked "Oficina Economica Cubana," Cuban Economic Office. Bernard Coard's trip to the Soviet Union and Eastern Europe in May and June 1980 -- the first public Grenadian effort to seek Soviet aid -- was portrayed as an economic mission. But his discussions were followed by the secret signing in Havana on October 27, 1980, of the first of the U.S.S.R.-Grenada military assistance agreements discovered in the wake of the collective action. This was eighteen months before the U.S.S.R. opened an embassy in Grenada. The documents also show that Grenadian contacts with the Soviet Union were handled primarily by Coard. Bishop, Army Commander Hudson Austin and lesser officials also were involved, but Bishop in particular had closer contacts with Cuba.

## The Soviet Bloc Role

East Germany was the most heavily involved of the Soviet bloc countries, providing several kinds of assistance. Documents confirm that East Germans were active in party, trade union and youth organizations, and provided equipment for security forces, including uniforms, bedding, knapsacks and pistols. The East Germans were also upgrading the island's telephone system.

Czechoslovakia supplied 3,000 assault rifles, 50 rocket propelled grenade launchers, and more than a million rounds of ammunition.

## North Korea

North Korea and Grenada announced a five-year development program during Prime Minister Bishop's trip to P'yongyang in April, 1983. According to the public announcement, North Korea would help build a 15,000-seat stadium, a party headquarters building, a fruit-processing factory, two fishing boats and an irrigation system. North Korea would provide technical advisors and some construction materials and equipment, while Grenada would provide the bulk of the labor and materials and pay for the expenses of the technicians.

During that same visit to P'yongyang, however, Bishop concluded a secret military assistance agreement in which North Korea promised to supply small arms, ammunition and equipment to equip a force of more than 1,000 men. This equipment, listed in the formal agreement at a value of $12 million, was to include 1,000 assault rifles, 80 machine guns, 50 portable rocket launchers, 2 coast guard patrol boats, 6,000 uniforms, and large amounts of ammunition and other equipment.

## The Cuban Presence

Cuban construction workers, other paramilitary personnel and regular military forces in Grenada outnumbered the total active strength of the Grenadian P.R.A. Cuban advisers held positions in all key ministries.

According to an official Cuban communique, 784 Cubans were on Grenada on October 25. The Cuban breakdown lists 636 as construction workers. Military and security personnel, not including a dozen crew members of two Soviet-built AN-26 transports, were listed as 53. Not counting Carlos Diaz of the American Department of the Cuban Communist Party (A.D.C.C.P.) diplomats were listed as 18. Other Cuban Ministries listed as having more than 6 persons on Grenada were Public Health, with 17, and Education, with 12.

Referring to the construction workers, Fidel Castro stated at his October 26 press conference that "of course, as workers, like all workers in Cuba, they have received military training."

Cuban workers constructed a battalion-sized military camp at Calivigny, less than five miles from the airport. The camp included a large training area and Soviet-style obstacle course. At Frequente, adjacent to the airport, a Cuban barracks had rifle racks down the center aisle.

The Cuban officer who had commanded the Cuban military mission in Grenada from 1981 until May 1983, Colonel Pedro Tortolo Comas, returned to command the Cuban-led resistance less than 24 hours before the landing of the U.S.-Caribbean security force. More than 40 Cuban military advisers on the scene were reporting to Havana through a Cuban vessel, the Viet Nam Heroico, stationed immediately outside St. Georges harbor. Relative to their numbers, the highest casualty rate was suffered by the Cubans who had been instructed by Fidel Castro to "fight to the death" in spite of U.S. assurances to Havana that all Cubans would be treated humanely and repatriated to Cuba as soon as practicable.

### The Weapons Actually Found

Large numbers of weapons, many still in crates, have been discovered on Grenada. The single largest concentration was at Frequente, which probably was the "central store room" referred to in several documents. There were six ware-houses at that site: one for arms; one for ammunition; and four for quartermaster items, spare parts and vehicles. Arms also were found at the Cuban Construction camp, Fort Rupert, Fort Frederick, Richmond Hill and many smaller caches.

### The Point Salines Airport

The precise purposes behind this military buildup remain unclear, but obstensibly civilian projects such as the extension to 9,000 feet of the runway at the point Salines Airport, and the Soviet study of the feasibility of a Grenadian port to service large deep-draft ships, had important military potential.

Cuba reached an agreement with Grenada in November 1979 to build a new airport in the Point Salines area of Southern Grenada. Before the month was out, a pilot team of 36 Cuban construction workers had arrived to begin the project. The following March, the Cuban merchant ship Playa Larga arrived in Grenada with heavy construction equipment and a brigade of 136 construction workers. By November, 1980, the total involved in building the airport had reached 300. According to the Cuban government communique cited earlier, the total in October, 1983, was 636.

While most Grenadian officials consistently denied that the Point Salines airport would serve any military purpose, the possibility of both Soviet and Cuban use was clearly envisaged. Selwyn Strachan, the Grenadian Minister of Mobilization, stated publicly in 1981 that Cuba would eventually use the new airport to supply troops in Africa, and that the U.S.S.R. would also find it useful because of its "strategic location" astride vital sea lanes and oil transport routes. An N.J.M. member who had received training in Moscow wrote in his personal notebook, apparently in October, 1983, that rumors were being spread that "the Party wanted Bishop to sign for the Airport to be a Military Base and he did do that." Finally, the Cuban motivation for constructing such a modern, all-weather airport must be assessed in light of the other Cuban activities on Grenada."₄

The P.R.G. was also concerned with developing the economic sector. Bishop said that his economic plans would be mainly concerned with increasing agricultural production, the fisheries industry and new tourism. In a November 23, 1981, address the Prime Minister said that his government had embarked upon both the diversification of agriculture and the establishment of new markets in an attempt to help build the nation's economy. Bishop also noted the strengthening of the tourist industry: "we have also been diversifying our tourist markets through increased promotion in Western Europe, the Caribbean and Latin American markets, while nonetheless attempting to maintain and indeed to achieve diversification in our traditional North American Market."₂

The revolution was further concerned with the following: reduction of the unemployment rate, improvement of the educational system, improvement of health facilities, transporation facilities and an improvement of sense of nationhood. According to the Prime Minister, unemployment had been reduced by 50 percent and working conditions for the workers were much improved.

To improve the educational system, the P.R.G. established a center for popular education, instituted a system of free secondary education, and created a national in-service teacher training program for the professionalization of all primary school teachers. The P.R.G. secured some 109 scholarships for university education for students in Grenada. They had also reduced school fees at the secondary schools by 25 cents per term and were able to provide hot lunches for quite a number of primary school students. The government's economic, education, military and agricultural programs, according to the P.R.G., were somewhat progressive and few Grenadians criticized the P.R.G. on these grounds. Their social programs, such as health social services, opportunities for women, and opportunities for the rural poor, on the other hand, were criticized by Grenadians at home and abroad.

The revolution did not develop as it was envisaged in the N.J.M.'s manifesto. Anthony P. Maingot was correct when he said that "the party's Central Committee, not any people's revolutionary armed forces... was trained and equipped by the Cubans. The East Germans trained the secret police. Rather than Village Assemblies, mass organizations were led by the inner circle. Rather than grass roots agricultural development, the P.R.G.'s energies were taken up by a major airport... A new blue print was revealing itself, a new description of Grenadian reality..."₅

An analysis of internal memoranda reveals that the revolution, in spite of the positive pictures that were painted by members of the N.J.M., the Central Committee, and the P.R.G., was not achieving its ideological mission. An interview with a former member of the P.R.A. in August of 1981 highlighted some of the problems that the P.R.G. faced. Mr. A.A., a former lieutenant in the P.R.A. and an influential member in the Central Committee told the authors that "the revolution is experiencing economical, social and ideological problems... Some of our members are forgetting the mission and purpose of the struggle. They are more concerned with building personal empires. I am concerned about this. I am, nevertheless, certain that the mission of the revolution would eventually be accomplished."₆ Mr. A.A. was annoyed when we asked him to explain what he meant by the mission of the revolution. Instead he said that the revolution is for food, work and democracy. It should be pointed out that members of the P.R.G., the N.J.M., and the P.R.A., and the Central Committee, when pressed for specific answers about the accomplishements and direction of the revolution, usually resorted to reciting phrases that had become part of the N.J.M.'s vocabulary.

Before we conclude this section, it might be helpful to highlight some of the events that preceded the house arrest of the Prime Minister, Maurice Bishop in 1983. On March 13, 1979, Gairy's government was toppled by Maurice Bishop and the N.J.M. while he was attending a meeting at the United Nations in New York. The constitution of Grenada was suspended and Bishop became the new Prime Minister. Several of Gairy's supporters and his entire Cabinet, except Derek Knight, were arrested. On November 22, 1979, Cuba increased aid to Grenada. Most of the aid came in the form of military hardware, teachers, doctors, and construction workers for the Point Salines airport. In May 1980, Bernard Coard, the Deputy Prime Minister, signed a treaty in Moscow permitting Soviet long-range reconnaissance planes to land at the new airport. In a

March 29, 1981 speech on Radio Free Grenada (R.F.G.), Bishop said "the United States understands the importance of our international airport..., and we as a people must therefore mobilize and fight back to defend our interest."[2] Reagan and the United States government opposed the construction of the 9,000-foot airfield and claimed that it would be used by Cuba and Russia to export revolution to the rest of the Caribbean islands. In a meeting of the Commonwealth Caribbean foreign ministers, Bishop charged that the United States was trying to overthrow his government and cited a "three stage CIA plot." On August 26, he charged that the U.S., and the North Atlantic Treaty Organization's (N.A.T.O.) military exercises in the Caribbean were a practice run for the invasion of Grenada.

On September 25, 1983, at a meeting of the Central Committee, Bishop was asked to share power with his Deputy, Bernard Coard. At that meeting Cde. Bernard said that he was shocked with Bishop's position because "it reveals a low ideological level and understanding..."[5] At another meeting of the Central Committee, October 12, 1983, Bishop was accused of spreading false rumors of a plot by Deputy Prime Minister Coard to kill him. It was at this meeting that the Central Committee agreed to place Bishop under house arrest. On October 13, the Grenada Prime Minister became the first head of government in the region to be placed under house arrest.

**A Chronology of the Grenada Revolution and Its Aftermath. Time-Frame Two: October 14, 1983 to October 23, 1983.**

**October 14, 1984:** The Deputy Prime Minister of Grenada, Bernard Coard, resigned to dispel rumors that he was involved in a plot to kill Prime Minister Maurice Bishop.[7,12] It is alleged that ideological differences and an internal power struggle between the two men,[8] which had been brewing since mid-1982, had smouldered into a situation of personal hatred and vengeance. Coard, also the country's Finance and Trade Minister as well as a hard-line Marxist,[7] accused Bishop of "not socializing the country faster and for encouraging the development of the private sector, which still controls some 60 percent of the nation's economy."[8] Bishop was also perceived by Coard as not being a "true revolutionary, and unwilling to participate in a situation of collective leadership."[9]

Ideological outlook between the two men created a split within the ranks of the N.J.M. Consequently, there were two separate political factions within the party. On the one hand, there was Bishop with his supporters in government; on the other, there was Coard with the support of governmental ministers who were opposed to the political views of Maurice Bishop. Not only was there a split within the ranks of the N.J.M., but Coard's faction functioned as a "semisecret factional grouping or clique... to strengthen its influence and control inside the government apparatus."[2] In other words, "it functioned more and more as a party within the party."[2]

Exacerbating the gap between the two men was the fact that Bishop, an alleged liberal Marxist, "had announced that preparation of a draft constitution had begun laying the groundwork for future island wide elections."[2] This move, on the part of the Prime Minister, had Coard believing that the former had intentions of reverting the country back to democracy. Coard was obviously infuriated over this alleged action, and was not prepared to let this happen. Therefore, he severed his ties with Bishop, thus ending a relationship that dated as far back as 1977. Indeed, political philosphies had escalated to a situation of personal vendetta[10] and it was precisely this existing state of affairs that had observers believing that Bishop might be killed by his own deputy.[11]

**October 15, 1983:** On this day, dissention within the hierarchy of the N.J.M. was confirmed. Reports began circulating that Prime Minister Maurice Bishop along with four Ministers in his government were placed under house arrest some two days earlier.[12] It was reported that the Commander of Grenada's 3,000 man Army, General Hudson Austin and Major Liam James, both of whom were loyal to and shared Coard's political views, were the key figures in Bishop's arrest.[9] [10] Despite the fact that Coard had allegedly resigned from political office the previous day, reports had it that he was the key figure in Bishop's arrest, and that both Austin and James were merely acting under his directives.

The internal power struggle within the ranks of the N.J.M. was amply confirmed by this event. It would seem that Coard, who had apparently quit his post the day before, quickly re-emerged as perhaps the most powerful person in the nation. This event clearly indicates that Bishop was regarded as an enemy of the people, and there might well have been plots to kill him. It also exposes the fact that the Army's loyalty resided with Coard's faction and not necessarily with Bishop's, and that the Army was now a force to be reckoned with.

Bishop's arrest had some repercussions. Although portrayed as an enemy of the people, at least by Coard's faction, the former still maintained political support from members of his own faction. It was reported that Industrialization and Finance Minister, Kendrick Radix, a member of Bishop's faction of the N.J.M., led some "300 protestors in St. Georges, threatening a general strike if Bishop is not released by Monday." [9] [10] [12]. However, despite Radix's threats, the Army, which was now in control, made no concessions to the former thus reducing the possibility that the release of Bishop might be imminent. In the wake of politcal upheaval, revolutionary fervour, and national chaos, Radix, utterly·powerless and fearful of the present regime, later resigned his post in despair. The power of Bishop's political faction thus appeared to be weakening or, at least, so it seemed.

**October 17, 1983:** Despite the arrest of Bishop a few days earlier, neither Coard, Austin, nor James, the core members of Coard's faction of the N.J.M. claimed responsibility for this action. It was not until October 17 that General Hudson Austin formally announced "that Bishop is under house arrest for opposing internal party changes." [12] Austin also confirmed earlier reports by publicly noting that Bernard Coard had taken control of the N.J.M. and that the latter was now in charge and actually running Grenada. [12] [14] Thus, Coard's faction appeared to be taking a firm grasp on the political reins of the country and was not about to relinquish or abdicate them without a test of strength with Bishop's faction.

**October 19, 1983:** The confrontation between the two dueling factions was at hand. Reports indicated that some 3,000 of Bishop's supporters took to the streets in a demonstration that culminated in his release. [12] [15] [16] Bishop and his supporters subsequently marched to Fort Rupert, the Army headquarters. Once there, they were surrounded by soldiers from the Army who were loyal to Coard and Austin. [12]

Then quickly, the soldiers began firing into the crowd of Bishop and his supporters. Prime Minister Bishop and a few Cabinet members were shot dead. [16] [17] [18] [19] [20] [21] Those killed were Foreign Minister Unison Whiteman, Housing Minister Norris Bain, and Education Minister Jacqueline Creft. [17] [18] [19] The casualty list also included seventeen dead and sixty-nine wounded. [12]

Following this bloody confrontation, a sixteen man Revolutionary Military Council (R.M.C.) was established with Coard, Austin and James as the key figures. [19] Austin, the Army Commander, grabbed the opportunity to make a public statement over Radio Free Grenada (R.F.G.) Austin told the Grenada citizenry that a "Revolutionary and Military Council had been established to rule the Caribbean island and that all schools and businesses will be closed until normality is returned... He said a 24-Hour curfew had been imposed until 6:00 p.m., Monday, that no one would be allowed to leave their homes, and that the armed forces were under 'strict instructions' to shoot anyone who seeks to disturb the peace."[17] [18] [19] [23] Austin also ordered that Grenada's leading airport, Pearls Airport, be closed indefinitely.[12]

**October 20-23, 1983:** On October 20, the R.M.C. proceeded to announce the dissolution of Bishop's regime, the P.R.G., and to dismiss all of its cabinet Ministers.[12] [27] The former also warned that the P.R.A. will fight to the last man against any foreign aggression.[12]

These events clearly indicate that Grenada was a country under siege. A power struggle between the two contending factions of the N.J.M. had been waged.[23] Not only was Prime Minister Bishop killed in a bloody confrontation, but his entire faction of the N.J.M. was forcefully ousted from political office. The R.M.C., with the support and loyalty of the Army, had decisively won the struggle. The R.M.C., therefore, controlled the political reins of the country and, for all essential purposes, was now sitting in the "driver's seat."

The existing state of affairs in Grenada was hardly welcomed by Caribbean countries and by the United States.[18] Caribbean heads of state and the United States criticized and condemned the actions of the newly formed R.M.C. that had so ruthlessly seized power.[18]

The fact that Grenada was now ruled by an orthodox Marxist regime elicited an increased interest in activities on the island. A Marxist government in Grenada posed a serious threat to the Caribbean in that it could, more than ever before, destabilize the region as a whole.[24] Thus, Caribbean leaders had a problem on their hands and, as the data shows, they were prepared to do something about it.

In an emergency meeting that took place in Port of Spain, Trinidad on October 22 and 23, 1983, leaders from thirteen Caribbean countries, all members of the Caribbean Common Market (C.A.R.I.C.O.M.), convened to discuss the Grenada crisis.[25] "Proposals were advanced to the meeting that were consistent with the established foreign policy" of Caribbean Nations "based on the priniciples of the United Nations Charter... The fundamental elements of this policy are non-interference in the internal affairs of other states and the avoidance of the use of force in the conduct of international relations and in the settlement of disputes."[26] The proposals were:

(i)    No involvement of any external elements in the resolution of the Grenada situation.

(ii)    The resolution of the Grenada situation should be wholly regional, that is to say CARICOM in nature.

(iii)    The regional solution pursued should not violate International Law and the United Nations Charter.

(iv)    Any proposed solution should have as its primary purpose the restoration of normality in Grenada. [26]

Leaders of CARICOM nations present at this meeting decided that, through contact with the Governor-General of Grenada, they would seek to accomplish the following:

(A)    The immediate establishment of a broad-base Civilian Government of National Reconciliation whose composition was acceptable to the Governor-General. The primary function of that government would be the putting into place of arrangements for the holding of elections at the earliest possible date;

(B)    Acceptance of a fact-finding mission comprising of eminent nations of CARICOM states;

(C)    The putting into place of 'arrangements to ensure the safety of nationals of CARICOM states;

(D)    The putting into place of arrangments to ensure the safety of nationals of other countries in Grenada and/or their evacuation where desired;

(E)    The acceptance of the deployment of a peace keeping force comprising of contingents contributed by CARICOM countries. [26]

Caribbean leaders took the political decision to expel Grenada from CARICOM and to support sanctions against Grenada. The proposed sanctions were as follows:

1.    No official contact with the existing regime.

2.    The regime would not be permitted to participate in the deliberations and business of the organization.

3.    Representatives of the regime would not be permitted to participate in or chair caucuses of groupings pertaining to meetings of International Agencies and would not be permitted to speak on behalf of the OECS in International Agencies.

4. The regime would not be allowed to benefit from the trade, economic and functional co-operation arrangements of the organizations.

5. No new issues of currency will be made to the regime under the Eastern Caribbean Central Bank (E.C.C.B.) arrangements.

6. The OECS Governments will cease all sea and air communication links with Grenada.[26]

In addition to collective sanctions imposed on Grenada by members of CARICOM, certain individual Caribbean countries imposed sanctions of their own. For example, in a nationwide broadcast, Jamaican Prime Minister Edward Seaga, condemned the military junta.[18] Seaga noted that "Jamaica will break diplomatic relations with the present Grenadian Government and will not consider a renewal of these relations until constitutional government has been restored..."[18 27]

Prime Minister George Chambers, speaking on behalf of the people of Trinidad and Tobago, joined this "sanction-imposing" list.[27 8] "Chambers announced that Trinidad and Tobago would not participate in any CARICOM meetings whatsoever in which Grenada would be present; no Grenada citizens or nationals would be allowed entry into Trinidad and Tobago without a visa; no exports from Grenada into Trinidad and Tobago would be afforded CARICOM treatment and no vessels registered in Grenada would be allowed the facilities of the CARICOM jetty in Trinidad and Tobago."[29]

The U.S. also condemned the activities in Grenada. Acting as a spokesman for the American people, President Reagan noted that Cuba and the Soviet Union were primarily responsible for the Grenadian coup. Both these countries "had indeed moved, with only modest investments of men and weaponry, to establish a puppet regime that would give them bases for other operations."[30] Reagan proceeded to voice concern over the lives of an estimated 1200 Americans living in Grenada. At this time, however, he mentioned nothing of a possible U.S. invasion of the island. What he did, in fact, was to dispatch promptly two United States diplomats to visit Grenada "to look into the safety of U.S. nationals living on the island."[31] The Reagan administration's concern over the safety of Americans living in Grenada was "prompted" by a telegram he received from parents of American students attending the St. George's Medical School on the island. "The telegram, signed by more than 500 parents, asked the President not to move too quickly or to take any precipitous and provocative actions at this time... 'Those are our children down there and we don't want them caught in any crossfire'..."₃₂

It is apparent from the preceeding discussion that both Caribbean countries and the U.S. were vehemently opposed to the on-going activities in Grenada. However, one point needs to be clarified. While it is true that Caribbean leaders were opposed to the Grenadian coup and had imposed sanctions against that country, they were also opposed to foreign invasion of the island. This fact was made abundantly clear by Caribbean leaders in the proposals they drew up at the Trinidad meeting.

This information is significant, because it serves to dispel rumors by the media that the CARICOM meeting in Trinidad was allegedly convened not only to discuss the Grenada crisis but also to request military assistance from the U.S., that is, to have the U.S. intervene militarily in the Grenada crisis, as it eventually did, in an attempt to restore normalcy to both the island and the region as a whole.

A word of caution ought to be exercised. While it is possible that a U.S. military intervention in the Grenada crisis may have been requested by CARICOM leaders it was, at least, not done so on the basis of consensus. In other words, Caribbean leaders did not collectively and agreeably ask the United States to invade the island. If anything, no action was taken and no decision reached at the CARICOM meeting in Trinidad regarding the issue of whether or not Grenada should be invaded.

The CARICOM meeting, as well as the concern for Americans living in Grenada, provided the Reagan administration an opportunity it was looking for. The former used both these issues as political ploys to focus attention on the island and to monitor happenings there. This observation is amply reinforced by the fact that the Reagan administration had contacted Prime Minister Tom Adams of Barbados concerning developments on the strife-torn island. Reagan had also earlier dispatched two U.S. envoys to Grenada. He obviously used both issues as good reasons - as good theoretical legitimate fronts - to have American personnel, military or otherwise, on Grenadian soil or close to it.

Historically, the U.S. has always monitored political events in the Caribbean. However, such monitoring was intensely escalated immediately following the overthrow of the Gairy government. Reports dating back to that period have indicated that Cuba and the Soviet Union had stepped up their activities in Grenada; and communism as a way of life was beginning to have a profound impact on Grenadian society.₃₃ It was precisely the "communist take-over" of the island and subsequent activities that prompted former U.S. President Jimmy Carter to take some action. In an article in the May 25, 1980 issue of the New York Times Magazine, it was noted: "The Carter Administration views the present trend as part of a broad Soviet offensive to win influence over the newly independent islands. The President has declared the Caribbean to be of 'extreme strategic importance' to the U.S. noting that social and economic discontent there had created an 'open avenue for Cuban adventurism' as well as 'the intrusion of outside forces.' Increasingly, it seems the Eastern Caribbean has become an element in the renascent cold war."[34] Carter proceeded to order "the establishment of a Caribbean Contingency Joint Task Force in Key West, Florida" to "employ designated forces for action if required."[34] The report continued by noting that "A 10-plane squadron of A-4 attack bombers were móved into the Key West Naval Air Station in April; and this will be strengthened soon by an additional seven aircrafts. Since January, a 20-plane Navy electronic-warfare squadron equipped for radar jamming has been stationed in Key West."[34] And, "in March, the aircraft carrier U.S.S. Nassau paid a 'show the flag' visit to the Eastern Caribbean."[34] "According to the United States intelligence experts, the Russians are planning extensive naval and air maneuvers in the region - an escalation of the existing pattern of warship visits to Cuba and flights by long range reconaissance aircraft."[34] Thus the military moves made by the U.S. were in "response to the suspected presence of a Soviet combat brigade on Cuban territory. In a broader sense, these measures were also triggered by the revolutionary trends in the Eastern Caribbean."[34]

The Reagan administration picked up where the Carter administration left off. In fact, the former escalated the monitoring of communist backed leftist activities in the Caribbean, and specifically in Grenada. It even went as far as actually conducting war exercises in the region.

In order to stop the alleged spread of communism in the Caribbean, "Washington was determined from day one to crush the Grenada revolution by armed might. The military and political groundwork for such aggression began to be paid by Carter's Democratic Party administration and continued under the Republican Reagan. U.S. military forces staged a trial run on a tiny island off Puerto Rico in 1981. This mock invasion was transparently named Operation Amber and the Amerdines, to echo the actual island chain of Grenada and the Grenadines. Even the pretexts for the practice invasion were the same as Reagan's phony justification in October 1983."[2]

Reports during Reagan's first term in political office indicated that the U.S. Congress also gave increasing attention to the situation in Grenada and stepped up action by formulating policies for the stabilization of the island.[35] Time Magazine reported that the Reagan administration was quite concerned about the East German, Libyan, Russian and Cuban presence on the island.[36] Of most concern was that, with the aid of Eastern bloc countries, Grenada was building a military airport under the disguise of that of a civilian one.[36] President Reagan viewed this move as one that was designed to use Grenada as a military base for Cuban and Russian exportation of communism to the Eastern Caribbean.

Aggravating this situation was that the Reagan administration was accused of planting C.I.A. spies in Grenada.[37] It was also accused of undermining and attempting to overthrow the P.R.G.[38] and for putting pressure on the European Economic Community (E.E.C.), the World Bank (W.B.), and the International Monetary Fund (I.M.F.) to deny funds to the island.[39] Suffice to say, the Reagan administration had had enough; its patience was wearing thin; it had to do something, and soon. It was not prepared to allow the completion of the airport that was being built in Grenada. The completion of the island's airport would have meant that both Cuba and Russia would be able to step up their activities on the island. Also with increased Cuban and Russian manpower and military hardware in Grenada, a U.S. invasion would be extremely difficult. In fact, it might even be too late. Grenada was a "ticking time bomb" that could have spelled disaster for the entire Eastern Caribbean. So the Reagan administration had to act and not with words. Of course it was thinking invasion. But when? It would seem that the stage had been set and it was only waiting for an opportune moment. As we shall see, the "Grenada Coup" presented the Reagan administration with that long-awaited moment.

## A Chronology of the Grenada Revolution and Its Aftermath.
## Time-Frame Three: October 24, 1983 to October 30, 1983.

As we noted earlier, the "Grenada Coup" presented President Reagan with an opportune moment for the U.S. to invade the island. Reagan, who for a long time was poised and waiting, quickly seized the opportunity and capitalized on it. On learning of the "Grenada Coup" Reagan, on October 24, the eve of the invasion, diverted from Lebanon to Grenada "a 10-ship U.S. military fleet carrying 1900 Marines and military personnel."[12] According to the U.S. Department of Defense

(D.O.D), the diversion of the U.S. fleet was "for possible aid in evacuating American citizens on the island... and to effect a departure of the Americans from Grenada, and to insure their security..."[32]

**October 24, 1983:** Although the United States claims that it had diverted its fleet merely to insure the safety of Americans, the new military junta of Grenada refused to view this action as just exactly that. The latter accused the U.S. of meddling in its interal affairs and for planning an invasion. It even warned Grenadians that a United States invasion might be imminent.[12 16 21 32] It also proceeded to ease the twenty-four hour curfew it had imposed earlier. Government offices began re-opening while schools remained closed.

Grenada's military junta's analysis of this situation was correct. Despite the U.S. denial, one could see that an invasion was imminent. On the eve of October 24, soldiers from the West Indian islands of St. Lucia, Antigua and Jamaica were seen landing at Barbados' Grantly Adams Airport. United States Marines, in full combat gear, also landed in Barbados. Later that day, the Marines, with military transport planes and transport and gunship helicopters, were seen taking off from the Barbados National Airport. (Grenada is approximately one hundred and fifty miles southwest of Barbados). Where were the Marines headed? Reports at the time speculated that they might have been headed for Grenada. These reports, as we know, were later confirmed. For all practical purposes, Barbados was used as a base for United States and Caribbean military operations. The invasion of Grenada was at hand.

**October 25-30, 1983:** On October 25, 2,000 U.S. and 300 Caribbean troops invaded Grenada.[12 40] R.F.G., President Reagan and Prime Minister Eugenia Charles of the Caribbean island of Dominica, later confirmed the invasion. Something should be noted here. Caribbean leaders who had earlier opposed foreign invasion of Grenada now militarily joined hands with the U.S. to overthrow Grenada's ruling n ilitary junta, the very thing they had earlier denounced. The fact that Barbados was used as a base for military operations by both the U.S. and Caribbean countries without any opposition from Caribbean leaders, clearly indicates that some Caribbean leaders, if not all, were in favor of using military action against Grenada. It also clearly exposes the fact that despite earlier statements to the contrary at the CARICOM meeting some Caribbean leaders must have, somewhere along the line, covertly asked President Reagan and the U.S. for military assistance.

Meanwhile, the invasion was a bloody one. It was marked by intense fighting and heavy casualty losses. Reports from U.S. ham radio operators in Grenada indicated that "the voices of the radio operators... were at times almost drowned out by the sound of artillery, anti-aircraft and small arms fire. The sounds of helicopters and jets could also be heard as they broadcast their accounts."[30] Several eye witnesses noted that "there's been no dropping of bombs yet, but four-engine aircraft and helicopter gunships have fired at the ground."[30] "There's sporadic sniper fire here and there" and there is "quite a bit of gunfire."[30] Reports also noted that on the first day of fighting, U.S. and Caribbean forces seized both the Pearls commerical airport and the Point Salines military airport that was allegedly under construction with Cuban and Russian aid. The latter was subsequently used as the headquarters for the multinational force.[30][40] As the invading troops advanced to the island's capital of St. George's, they were resisted by Grenadian and Cuban troops. More intense fighting ensued as "United States troops battled... soldiers and militiamen in congested neighborhoods of the capital."[41] The leftist forces pressed their resistance in the capital, but were quickly overcome by the multinational force.[40][41] Some thirty Cuban soldiers were killed and six hundred were seized. An undisclosed number of Grenadian soldiers were also killed. Thirty Soviet advisors to the Grenadian government were also seized. On the other hand, casualty losses on the part of the U.S., at this stage, stood at "six killed, eight missing and 33 wounded."[41] There was no information on civilian casualties.

While most of the heavy fighting was now over, this cessation in battle suggests that the invasion itself was not completely over. News bulletins indicated that Cuban workers and helpers continued their resistance against American forces and held the latter at bay for about a day. There was also some strong resistance by General Hudson Austin's men who were hiding in the hills and engaging the American forces in a type of guerila warfare. In the process, the American forces suffered additional loss of life and limb. The casualty list at this point: "11 American soldiers reported dead, 67 wounded and 7 missing."[43]

The resistance by the leftist forces was not long-lived. Despite increasing casualty losses, American forces kept pressing on and soon overcame their oppositon. In fact, Bernard Coard, the hard-line Marxist and one of the engineers of the Grenada coup, was captured on October 29 .[44] The following day, General Hudson Austin, one of the key figures in the ruling military junta and chief of the leftist forces, was also seized by U.S. forces.[45] Both leaders were now in custody, and thus unable to give directions to the leftist guerilas. Not having a second line of leadership to continue the struggle, the leftists surrendered to American forces. Although there were some intermittent and occasional sniper firings subsequent to this period the American invasion of Grenada, for all practical purposes, was essentially over. The United States had decisively won the struggle; it had successfully put down this uprising by armed insurgents and leftist dissident political factions. The former had convincingly defeated Grenada's revolutionary ruling military junta who, with the aid of Cuba and Russia, had ruthlessly deposed Prime Minister Maurice Bishop from power in a bloody coup a few days earlier.

The news of American military success in Grenada was generally welcomed in the U.S. The U.S. Department of Defense claimed that the Marines and the Rangers quickly achieved their initial goals. President Reagan insisted that the positive rather than the negative elements of the invasion should be emphasized. In a Columbia Broadcasting System (C.B.S.) news poll, 51 percent of Americans approved of the President's action on the invasion while 37 percent disapproved. Congratulatory messages poured into the White House from Americans all over the country indicating that they were proud to be Americans. To many Americans and Grenadians, the Reagan administration was, after all, standing tall. It was a victory for democracy. Ronald Reagan had, indeed, decisively stopped both the entrenchment and spread of communism in the Eastern Caribbean.

In a series of press interviews which followed the invasion, Ronald Reagan defended his decision to invade Grenada. He noted that his decision to invade Grenada which was made on October 22 and 23 while playing golf, was necessary to forestall what was considered a "Cuban arms buildup."[41] He also confirmed that his decision was prompted by a request from leaders of five Caribbean countries, including Grenada's Governor General Sir Paul Scoon, asking him to intervene in the crisis in an attempt to restore stability to the region.[30][46] It must be noted that Ronald Reagan's confirmation of being asked by Caribbean leaders to intervene in the Grenada crisis served to dispel a controversy surrounding this issue. From what we know now, the U.S. was asked to intervene - but certainly not by all the CARICOM countries that had earlier convened at the Trinidad meeting. This indicates that Caribbean leaders themselves were divided on the issue of whether or not Grenada should be invaded.

A point ought to be noted here and that is "despite its claims that it was invited into Grenada by the Organization of Eastern Caribbean

States, Prime Minister Tom Adams of Barbados admitted that the O.E.C.S. governments were contacted about the operation by U.S. officials at the time Bishop's house arrest first became known."[2] This point amply confirms that the United States invasion of Grenada was not only prompted by a request from Caribbean leaders, but also because of the former's concern for activities on the island during this period. President Reagan's contact with Prime Minister Tom Adams over the existing state of affairs on the island, subsequent to Bishop's house arrest, attests to this fact.

The Reagan administration's moment of glory in the face of U.S. military success was thwarted by criticisms from the international community. In Grenada, Charles R. Modica, Chancellor and founder of St. George's University School of Medicine, levied harsh criticism against the President for invading the island and for "acting on the wrong advice."[30] Modica commented further that the lives of American medical students attending St. George's University were not in any danger despite Ronald Reagan's alleged insistence to the contrary. In fact, the former insisted that Grenada's ruling military junta had assured him that the lives of American students on the island were not in jeopardy.

The Soviet Union and Premier Fidel Castro of Cuba were also quick to blast the Reagan administration. In addition to accusing the U.S. of firing at its embassy in Grenada, Russia referred to Ronald Reagan as a "latter-day Napolean for the 'feat' of seizing tiny Grenada with a United States Armada."[47] Russia also called the invasion "a crime against peace and humanity"[41] and assailed the move on the part of the U.S. as "undisguised banditry."[30] Meanwhile, Cuban Premier Fidel Castro "denounced the invasion", and condemned it as "imperialist Yankee aggression."[41]

Criticisms also poured in from the Organization of American States (O.A.S.). Reports indicated that "most delegates to the Organization of American States condemned the invasion of Grenada... as a violation of international law and the principle of non-intervention in the affairs of member states."[41]

Countries from N.A.T.O. disapproved of the U.S.' actions. In an article in The New York Times, it was noted that many of the U.S. allies criticized the American invasion of Grenada.[41] The same article pointed out that "Britain, France and Italy have all expressed criticism of the Grenada operation."[41] For example, the Italian view was "we are against military intervention for the solution of international controversies...

Prime Minister Margaret Thatcher intervened by telephoning President Reagan in an effort to stop the invasion... The French Government later issued a statement condemning the attack... The West Germans have also told Washington of their unhappiness with the invasion... as have the Canadians."[41]

Criticisms ran the entire gamut; both U.S. allies and non-allies were involved. The Reagan administration was standing tall a while earlier; now it was standing alone, it would seem. Understandably, the former expected criticism from non-allies, but not from allies whose interests are somewhat synonymous with those of the U.S. and which, for the most part, should have been compatible with the aims of the invasion. In any event, Ronald Reagan had already acted and the U.S. military operation in Grenada was virtually already over. The 1983 Grenada invasion was now history and Ronald Reagan had to prepare himself to face the consequences of his action; he had to prepare himself to face the pressure from the international community.

But the Reagan administration's woes were not yet completely over. If anything, his administration had much more dissention to contend with. Such dissention was not foreign in nature but, instead, it came from within the ranks of the U.S. government itself, and from groups and organizations within the country. On October 26, a number of the democratic party leaders in Washington moved on the War Power's Act (W.P.A.). They charged that "the Reagan Administration had not complied with the War Power's Resolution (W.P.R.) when ordering the invasion of Grenada."[41] Under the W.P.R. the President must inform the Congress of an invasion. The President must also "...withdraw the troops within 60 days unless Congress authorizes them to stay longer."[41] Ronald Reagan did not inform the Congress of his action until after the invasion. The New York Times reported that he later sent a letter to "congressional leaders outlining his reasons for invading Grenada."[41] However, in that letter he indicated that American forces "will remain only so long as their presence is required,"[41] but insisted that "the law cannot tie his hands as Commander in Chief."[41]

Ronald Reagan was talking tough. Despite an outpouring of criticisms, he viewed his action as proper and necessary, and was willing to defend it. As Commander in Chief, he was prepared to use, or maybe even abuse, the power of his political office. He was determined to silence his opponents despite their increasing opposition.

Reports at the time also noted that the United States Congress was divided in terms of how it viewed the invasion. Some members of Congress were in favor of the invasion while others were against it. Those in support of it might have provided the President some solace and reaffirmed his decision to invade.

Criticisms also emerged from within the ranks of the Black community. According to the Amsterdam News, the Congressional Black caucus condemned the invasion, charging that President Reagan ordered the attack on Grenada because the island's inhabitants were Black and defenseless. Religious and civil rights leaders also made their feelings known by noting that "deliberate intervention by the Reagan administration in the affairs of a sovereign nation under the guise of protecting U.S. citizens is a blatant violation of international law."[43]

The events at the United Nations (U.N.) headquarters in New York were also clearly in opposition to the invasion. At the Dag Hammarskjold Plaza, more than 2500 people rallied to express opposition to the invasion. Protesters pleaded for non-intervention and withdrawal of American troops.

But there were additional events at the U.N. Both Nicaragua and Cuba requested "an urgent meeting of the Security Council to discuss the invasion of Grenada by American and Caribbean Troops."[48] The New York Times reported that Nicaragua "was expected to press for a resolution condemning the invasion."[49]

When the Security Council met later, the atmosphere was hectic and full of rage. The vast majority of nations represented at the U.N. condemned the invasion.[50] Criticisms were especially harsh from the socialist and communist bloc countries. Both aligned and non-aligned nations belonging to this organization viewed the U.S.' actions as unwarranted and termed them "deplorable".

The Reagan administration had one final issue to be concerned about during this period. It was the issue of American reporters who were barred by American forces in Grenada from entering that country to cover the invasion. It should be noted that immediately following the arrest and execution of Prime Minister Bishop, the ruling R.M.C., then in power, had expelled American reporters from the island. This meant that despite freedom of the press on the part of the American news media as well as the importance of the story, the American news media was shut out from the scene of action and, thus, unable to report on the invasion. Most of the coverage on the invasion was done by American military personnel manning ham radios, and by "foreign" journalists.

American reporters were obviously infuriated about this particular happening. They accused the Reagan administration of being in collusion with the military in taking this action, and in specifically having U.S. forces in Grenada forcefully deny them access to cover the invasion. The powerful U.S. media, therefore began raising questions about both the legality and implications of this action. Countering the media's allegations, the Reagan administration, in conjunction with the military, finally relented somewhat and allowed controlled coverage of the situation in Grenada, but only after most of the heavy fighting was over. For example, in an October 28 New York Times article titled "U.S. Allows 15 Reporters to Go to Grenada for Day" it was noted, "the Reagan Administration permitted a small group of reporters to go to Grenada today for the afternoon as a furor continued over the limitations imposed on news coverage of the invasion of the tiny Caribbean island."[51] The article continued, "all reporters will have to return... on the same day."[51] Indeed the limitations imposed on reporters had sparked a controversy between the White House and the U.S. media; to Reagan's supporters it was just yet another "fly in the ointment" that was able to thwart and undermine the popularity of Ronald Reagan and his administration in the face of a recent successful military operation. In any event, though, the ban imposed on U.S. reporters was considered necessary and desirable by the U.S. administration and the latter was prepared to defend it despite increasing criticism. It was designed to impose a "news blackout" on the Grenada situation or, at least, limit, screen, and filter whatever information that was reported concerning the invasion. As we shall see, the banning of U.S. reporters from Grenada was, at least, one reason why the U.S. military operation on that island was successful. More importantly, it helps the reader to understand why, in part, the Grenada revolution failed.

Meanwhile, by October 31, 1983, back in Grenada things were returning to normal. The heavy fighting was over but U.S. forces still stood on guard. Zones where there was intense fighting a few days earlier were now settling down to routine daily activity. There was, however, some sporadic firing from Cubans holding out in the hills and forests.[52] It was also reported that there was some looting of stores, as food supplies remained a problem. American troops also guarded check points and patrolled the city. For the most part though, electricity, water, and telephone service had been restored. Sir Paul Scoon, the Governor General, "asked Grenadians to open their shops, return to work, and send their children to school."[52]

A transition had indeed taken place. In fact, it was due to this apparent transition that "prospects for an early withdrawl of the bulk of United States Forces from Grenada" were improved.[52] The Department of Defense later issued a statement indicating that the Marines who invaded Grenada were set to resume their journey to Lebanon and they would be leaving in the next few days.

## A Chronology of the Grenada Revolution and Its Aftermath.
## Time-Frame Four: October 31 to Today

**October 31 - November 8, 1983:** Repercussions of the Grenada invasion continued to haunt the Reagan administration. For example, the American Society of Newspaper Editors (A.S.N.E.) joined reporters in taking action by protesting to the Defense Department "over its refusal to permit reporters to cover the first stages of the invasion...,"[53] and the House of Representatives listened to criticisms from both legal and media experts condemning the government for the barring of news coverage of the Grenada invasion. The U.N., too, adopted a resolution deeply deploring the armed intervention in this Caribbean island by United States forces. Despite the element of elapsing time which was contributing to a gradual decrease on the impact of the invasion, the Reagan administration's woes were not completely over. In fact, this was amply revealed as dissention within the ranks of the Reagan administration itself began surfacing. The White House reported that President Reagan's Deputy Press Secretary resigned "citing damage to his credibility resulting from the administration's handling of the Grenada invasion."[53]

In the face of adversity, the Reagan administration decided to reaffirm its earlier position by again defending its action in Grenada. President Reagan insisted that the action taken was necessary. He told news reporters that "we had conducted a rescue mission", and not an invasion.[53] He insisted that the word "invasion" had been frequently used by the media to refer to the Grenada operation, but this was not appropriately used.

In any event, though, President Reagan's reaffirmation of the action he had taken received tacit support from medical students who were evacuated from Grenada, and from the Speaker of the House of Representatives, Tip O'Neil, who was speaking on behalf of both the House of Representatives and the Democratic party. This support eventually began filtering down to the American public as a whole, and ultimately culminated in the easing of pressure that was earlier put on the shoulders of the U.S. President. Thus, the Reagan administration began restoring some of the credibility it seemed to have lost, at least from within the confines of the U.S.

Meanwhile the situation in Grenada was gradually being restored to normal. The wounded were evacuated and all captives, particularly Cubans, were repatriated. The island's Governor General, Sir Paul Scoon, also severed diplomatic relations "with Cuba, Libya and the Soviet Union."[54]

**November 9 and Beyond:** Following the U.S. intervention, a key issue of concern for Grenadians was, who was going to run the country? It must be remembered that the political machinery of both Maurice Bishop and Bernard Coard had been forcefully dismantled. This meant that the country had no official political body to oversee its daily activities. Other than a handful of U.S. forces and Governor General Sir Paul Scoon, the only civilian authority on the island, there was no legislative and /or political body to formulate and execute policies and act in the interests of the nation as a whole. In other words, there was simply no government. Grenada was, thus, in a vulnerable position. This situation obviously warranted the immediate appointment of a political body and/or interim government.

Steps were quickly taken in this direction. On November 9, 1983, nine Grenadians were named by Governor General  Sir Paul Scoon, to serve as an interim government and to prepare for elections.[55] While Scoon noted that the primary task of this body would be to prepare for elections, he was unwilling to indicate a date such elections were to take place. It would seem that Scoon wanted to maintain the political reins of the country for as long as he could in an attempt to restore political stability on the island. Added to this fact, of course, was the realization that he had the backing of the U.S. in his effort to realize this goal.

While Scoon had earlier declared that "he was not consulting with Americans on the formulation of his new government" yet, according to the Barbados Advocate "he reiterated that he had requested U.S. help" in some of the activities that were taking place on the island during this period.[56] While he made no specific mention of U.S. aid in his appointment of the interim government, it is rather difficult to believe that the U.S. was not asked for support or, to say the least, was not consulted in this matter, particularly given its military, socio-economic and political presence on the island then. While it was not overtly stated, one would suspect that there was some collusion on the part of the Governor General and the U.S. in the appointment of this interim government. Furthermore, given the existing state of affairs in Grenada during this time, it is quite likely that no action was ever taken by the Governor General without consultation with the U.S. We can discern this from precedents that were already set and, as we shall see, from events that were to follow.

As we noted earlier, the period of November 9, 1983, and beyond was one that was also concerned with ridding the society of socialist elements and reinstating a capitalist mode of production. Let us remember that a few days earlier Governor General Scoon had severed diplomatic relations with the communist bloc. This action was merely in conformity with and adherence to the aims of the invasion. Scoon, with the blessings and backing of the U.S., was prepared to use whatever force necessary to "dismantle every trace of political, social and economic accomplishments"[2] that the Bishop regime had tried to establish: he was firmly prepared "to wipe out all vestiges of the revolution"[2] and to keep it that way even if he had to use military force. Clearly, the U.S. had established a government that would act in and be subservient to its socio-economic and political interests.

But who were the targets of attack in this joint operation by the U.S. and the puppet government in their attempt to wipe out residues of socialism? "The central targets have been the cadres of the New Jewel Movement and mass organizations, whose consciousness remains the most durable conquest of the revolution. The occupiers are carrying out a most systematic effort to intimidate and break these cadres, who numbered in the tens of thousands, especially in the working class and among the youth."[2]

The attempt to dismantle socialism as a way of life in Grenada began with the invasion on October 25th and has been continuing ever since. Since the invasion, there has been the "arrest, detention, and grilling of more than 2,000 Grenadians."[2] Furthermore, those who were jailed and released have been "given cards warning them to refrain from participating in any anti-government activities."[2] An unknown number were also jailed indefinitely. Many surviving members of the N.J.M. have also been picked up by the authorities and detained for questioning. These political figures have been asked not to denounce the invasion - a charge that has been levied against them.

Government employees, too, have been the subject of repression. A purge and blacklist of government employees has been enacted based on C.I.A. computer printouts and political rights curtailed.[2]

Today, the process of the input of a capitalist mode of production in Grenada is most visible. Since the invasion and subsequent establishment of an interim government, there has been an outpouring of monies into Grenada by foreign nations whose political and economic orientations are established on the basis of democracy and capitalism. News reports have indicated that the U.S. is committed to a long-range rebuilding of Grenada. Since the invasion, the U.S. has poured huge sums of money into the island. It was reported that "the Reagan administration announced a $30 million package... of long term military and economic aid."[57] Half of these monies "would be used to revive the island's economy, repair roads, rehabilitate social services and expand agricultural projects. The rest would be spent to train and equip a 350-member Caribbean security patrol that will maintain order on the island after American troops leave."[57] Circulated reports also noted that the level of planned U.S. aid was supplemented by British and Canadian money.[58] Reports also noted that the interim Grenadian government had asked the government of Trinidad and Tobago (T&T) for a $10 million grant,[59] and had requested aid from both the International Monetary Fund (I.M.F.)[60] and the United States Peace Corps. On the business front, American capitalists have begun resuming business transactions with the island.[61] Airlines, too, are once again flying and tourism, which was one of the economic mainstays of the island prior to the People's Revolution in 1979, is again beginning to flourish. Capitalism is beginning to become the dominant economic mode and is gradually establishing a stronghold on the island.

Since the '79 Revolution and the U.S. invasion of the island, Grenada continues to rebuild. How long this process will take is anyone's guess. One thing is clear though, and that is that the American presence on the island in terms of economic aid, political stability, and protection from infiltration and domination by communist bloc nations will be visible for quite some time to come.

Today, the long road to the rebuilding of Grenada continues. The revolution which Maurice Bishop had successfully created nearly five years ago, as well as the coup that followed, was crushed by the armed might of the U.S. Thus, for all essential purposes, the revolution was over or, at least, so it seemed.

The country has once more adopted the Westminister form of government. On December 3, 1984, Grenadians elected a new government. The New National Party (N.N.P.) headed by Herbert A. Blaize, won 14 of the 15 political seats in the first national general elections since the overthrow of Eric Matthew Gairy in March of 1979. The G.U.L.P., Gairy's political party, won 1 seat and received 35 percent of the popular vote. The Maurice Bishop Patriotic Movement (M.B.P.M.) polled a mere 4.9 percent of the popular vote.

What does this election mean for Grenadians? While it may be somewhat early to analyze the impact of the general election on the future of Grenada it is, nevertheless, clear that Grenadians favor democracy over the Marxist/Leninist form of government. This seems to support the fact that one of the main reasons why the Grenada revolution failed was because of the political system Maurice Bishop opted for. In order for any government in Grenada to succeed, it must form alliances with the landed aristocracy, the old English aristocrats, the new middle classes, the workers (both from the town and country), and the religious institutions. A democratic or socialist form of government will not succeed if it seeks to play one group against the other. The N.N.P., if it intends to rule Grenada successfully, must represent every segment of the population. The results of the December 3, 1984 election indicate that the N.N.P., a merger of three political parties - the Grenada National Party, (G.N.P.); the Grenada Democratic Movement, (G.D.M.); and the National Democratic Party, (N.D.P.) - was supported by the business elite, the landed gentry, and the new middle classes. The majority of the working class, especially those from the countryside, supported Gairy. Therefore, one of the major tasks of the N.N.P. is to win the support of the working class.

Another major challenge to the new Prime Minister, Herbert Blaize, is to minimize internal conflicts that may arise from within the ranks of the N.N.P. The data we have suggests that the N.N.P. will, as the P.R.G. did, experience political conflict over matters of ideology and leadership in the party. It is public knowledge that certain members of the N.N.P. supported the P.R.G. and its Marxist/Leninist form of government. It is further known that the merger of the three political parties occured with the expressed purpose of defeating the G.U.L.P. Now that this objective is accomplished, where does Grenada go from here? One thing is certain and that is that no amount of American aid will solve the political, social, and developmental problems that face Grenada. Grenadians must be given the freedom and leeway to solve their own internal problems. Outside interference will simply do more harm than good. Grenadians, if they will work together for the good and welfare of the nation, are capable of managing their own affairs. The N.N.P. must insure that no Grenadian becomes a stranger or "slave" in his own country. Therefore, foreign investments, foreign aid, and foreign interference must be carefully guarded and controlled.

# CHAPTER FOUR

# IDEOLOGY AND
# THE GRENADA REVOLUTION

## Introduction

This chapter will examine and analyze the ideology of the Grenada revolution and note its meaning for the masses. It will then be possible to discern the impact of that ideology on the failure of the revolution.

The impact of a particular ideology on the development and outcome of a revolution cannot be denied. Ideology can determine both the extent to which mass support is mobilized, and the ultimate success or failure of that revolution.,When it can arouse them emotionally and reflect their overall interests and aspirations, ideology tends to bring people together and demand a commitment to action., Thus a comprehensive ideology that is reflective of the interests and aspirations of all concerned accomplishes the support of the masses and enhances its chances of success.,

But ideology can also inhibit mass mobilization and a commitment to action., In fact, it can sometimes culminate in the failure of a revolution. This is especially so when, after it is instituted, it fails to fulfill it's promised goals and does not develop organs of popular support from both the masses as well as from certain key figures who constitute an integral part of the hierarchy of leadership of the revolution itself.

Based on this theoretical premise, this chapter argues that the ideology of the Grenada revolution was partly responsible for its failure. The introduction of this ideology into Grenadian society, prior to and immediately following the overthrow of Eric Gairy by Maurice Bishop in 1979, was marked by an initial widespread acceptance of it by both the Grenadian masses and other leaders of the N.J.M. However, its repressive hand, its inability to live up to its promises, and its failure to fulfill the aspirations and expectations of the Grenada citizenry, were factors that culminated in a degree of alienation of Grenadians from it. Moreover, it was responsible for the creation of a serious ideological split between the two most important leaders of the N.J.M., - a split that subsequently intensified and was exacerbated to the point where it culminated in the overthrow of the Bishop regime by a military junta that emerged from within the ranks of the N.J.M. itself.

The ideology of the Grenada revolution will be viewed from the perspective of an examination and analysis of the following questions: (1) Who were the key political figures of the N.J.M.? (2) What were their respective ideologies? (3) How applicable were these ideologies to the masses of Grenadians and to Grenadian society on the whole? (4) And how did this ideology contribute to the failure of the revolution?

Let us recall that the N.J.M. was the main political arm of the revolutionary process in Grenada. Let us also recall that it was the N.J.M. that had forcefully deposed Eric Gairy and had come to control the political reins of the country. More importantly, it was both Maurice Bishop and Bernard Coard, the core political figures of the N.J.M., that were primarily responsible for the formulation of the N.J.M.'s ideological outlook. Thus, any examination and analysis of the ideology of the Grenada revolution and its applicability to Grenadian society as such must revolve around the N.J.M. as well as the different political preoccupations of these two men.

**The Ideology of Maurice Bishop and the N.J.M.**

The ideology of Maurice Bishop and the N.J.M. can be viewed from a number of perspectives. In the first place, according to Bishop, the N.J.M. really received its initial political thrust from the concerns of "Black Power" and the international Black Power Movement that was engulfing the world in the late sixties and early seventies. Before we discuss why Bishop embarked upon this ideology it is, however, important that we first briefly outline the history and meaning of this global ideology.

The term "Black Power" was coined by American Black Power advocate Stokeley Carmichael in 1966. Carmichael wrote, "Black Power is a call for Black people... to unite, to recognize their heritage, to build a sense of community... a call for Black peoples to begin to define their own goals, to lead their own organizations, and to support these organizations... a call to reject the racist institutions and values of this society."[2]

Following David Nicholls, Mahin Gosine notes that this concept of Black Power, first popularized in the U.S. in the late sixties, was hostile to widespread racial discrimination. During and after that period, the word "Black" referred to anyone of African descent, largely because of the undisputed influence of the writings of many Black intellectuals who equated the word "Black" with the African. As the Black Power Movement spread across the world, and particularly in the U.S. where it developed its momentum, it remained "Afro-centered" or more specifically, "Negro-centered."[3]

As we noted earlier, the Black Power Movement was not confined to the U.S.; the movement quickly spread to many other countries of the world such as Africa, England and the Caribbean where significant parts of the population are Black.

In the Caribbean, the Black Power Movement had a particularly profound impact. In 1968, the Caribbean's chief theoretician on the subject, Walter Rodney, began preaching revolutionary Black Power to the Caribbean masses, and advocating sweeping revolutionary changes for societies in that region. By 1970, Rodney's ideas had permeated all levels of Caribbean society. Later that year, there were mass uprisings in Trinidad as the 1970 Black Power Movement in that country came close to toppling the then fourteen-year regime of the late Prime Minister Dr. Eric Williams.[1]

But the Black Power Movement that erupted in Trinidad quickly spilled over in neighboring Grenada, where the vast majority of the population is Black. Large sections of the Grenadian masses who were already receptive to the ideas of Rodney, took to the streets in support of their Trinidad "brothers". Among them was Maurice Bishop.

Subsequent to him co-founding the N.J.M. and later becoming Prime Minister, Bishop held dearly to the ideals of Black Power as initially defined by Carmichael and later by Rodney. He firmly believed that the Black masses of the Caribbean had long been the victims of colonialist repression,[4] and that the local Caribbean leaders were merely "lackeys of imperialism" who were simply perpetuating colonial interests at the expense of locally oppressed peoples. Bishop also believed that historically, White colonial societies had exploited the wealth of Black societies like Grenada, and no longer could this be tolerated.

For Bishop, Black Power meant throwing off white domination, thus breaking the colonial economic stranglehold on underdeveloped Black societies like Grenada. It also meant a call to Grenadians to recognize their heritage and to identify proudly with it, to build a sense of community, and to begin to chart their own destinies.

The second aspect of Bishop's ideology was that it was firmly revolutionary.[5] Let us recall that subsequent to its formation, one of the first concerns of the N.J.M. was to establish a revolutionary government. The N.J.M. was clearly opposed to the Gairy regime: its primary concern was to take power by whatever means possible. In fact, in March 1979, Bishop and the N.J.M. had forcefully overthrown the Gairy regime, and had thus clearly taken power through the revolutionary method. Bishop's endorsement of the revolutionary process was amply confirmed by his actions: he continously explained to the Grenadian masses that the revolutionary course of action as pursued by the P.R.G. was both vital and necessary for the liberation of the people of that Caribbean nation. He even noted that no revolution has the right to consider itself a revolution if it does not have the capacity to defend itself. To him, the P.R.G.'s concern was to create a formidable militia so that Grenadians would be able to defend and protect the revolution they fought so intensely to bring about in 1979.

In the third place, the ideology Maurice Bishop succumbed to was anti-imperialist and anti-capitalist.[6] The ideas of this popular uprising -an uprising equated with and influenced by both the Cuban and the Nicaraguan revolutions that preceded it - were to throw off White imperial domination, and break the stranglehold bourgeois and colonial elements had on the society. This release would ultimately reduce contlict between and among Grenadian workers and help the P.R.G. to create national class solidarity and, thus, bring these working class factions under its hegemony.

The mobilization of the Grenadian working class to fight imperial and bourgeois elements was one of the fundamental principles of the N.J.M. It was a necessary prerequisite to accomplish the transition of a nation controlled by these elements to one controlled by the workers and the state political apparatus. Bishop envisioned that the Grenadian revolution would have much in common with the Cuban Revolution in that it will be the peasants and laborers who would eventually benefit from changes in the political and socio-economic infrastructure. As Bishop put it, it was with the help of the working people that the revolution was created, and it was with them that the island would advance to socialism.

The fourth element in Maurice Bishop's ideology was that it was

Marxist/Leninist in perspective. Following the teachings of both Marx and Lenin, Bishop attempted to make working class Grenàdians more aware of their class position. His goal was to educate them about the hazards of occupying the lower rungs of the socio-economic ladder in a stratified society. He also wanted to mobilize the people in an attempt to displace imperial political dictators and replace them with what the Marxists and Leninists referred to as the "dictatorship of the proletariat - that is, political rule by, and in the class interests of, the workers and poor farmers, the laboring majority.", Thus, Bishop wanted to break the economic power of the capitalists who controlled the society; he wanted to transform it in such a way so that it would be the working people who would ultimately reap the societal benefits.

The final and perhaps the most important element contained in Bishop's ideology was that of socialism. The N.J.M. leader referred to socialism, or "scientific socialism" as he specifically called it, as the "final victory" of the Grenada revolution. Scientific socialism was basically a political system instituted by socialist countries of the western world such as Cuba and Nicaragua whereby which the masses would carry out a "transition from the domination of capitalist property relations to the establishment of a workers state based on a state owned industry, economic planning, and a government monopoly of foreign trade.", Bishop argued that the N.J.M. initially started and later developed as a political party that was committed to following the dictates of scientific socialism. He warned that while he was aware that Grenada was a poor and backward country, and it would be difficult to resist the political and economic pressures that the imperial world of capitalism would bring to bear on it, yet it was important to develop strong ties with the socialist world for the adoption of socialism. Socialism, in itself, was a real possibility in Grenada- in fact, it was the only possibility for the true liberation of the masses, particularly the working class. The only way to rebuild Grenadian society and to accomplish true national liberation was to adopt the principles of scientific socialism. As far as Bishop was concerned, socialism was the only solution to Grenada's problems: it was the only alternative for the future of the country.

**The Ideology of Maurice Bishop and the N.J.M.: Its Meaning for and Applicability to Larger Grenadian Society.**

The ideology of Maurice Bishop and the N.J.M., particularly the preponderant element of scientific socialism, must be viewed from the perspectives of both its achievements, as well as its failures.

**Bishop's Achievements:** According to the N.J.M. and its supporters, the ideology as embarked upon by Maurice Bishop was responsible for effecting a number of positive changes within Grenadian society.[8] These changes and their applicability to Grenadian society will now be discussed.

Ever since his initial advent to political power in early 1979, Bishop began dismantling every aspect of the socio-economic and political infrastructure that ex-dictator Eric Gairy had tried to create, and began instituting his own.[9] One of the first things Bishop's new government attempted to do was to establish an army - a militia to defend the revolution. "Naturally, like other countries, we do have an army," he said. "It is a Grenadian army. Our security services are designed to protect and defend our people... and our revolution."[9]

Bishop's most significant achievements, claimed the N.J.M., were within the economic sector. Until March 1979, unemployment ran 50 percent; among women it was 69 percent, and among young people under 25 years of age it was 80 percent.[10] However, by mid-1983, four years after the revolution, unemployment had dropped to 12 percent.[10] In 1977 and 1978, laws passed by the Gairy regime banned industrial action by eleven categories of workers; and in practice, unionization of workers was subject to harassment, so that only 30 percent of workers, the majority of them male were members of trade unions.[10] Under Bishop, it is alleged that new laws were passed which made it mandatory for employers to recognize unions as well as employees' right to strike. Consequently, the membership of the island's trade unions rose from a mere 30 percent under Gairy to about 90 percent under Bishop.[7] Moreover, in 1982 the nation's Gross National Product (G.N.P.) grew by nearly 6 percent, accounting for a total of roughly 14 percent since the N.J.M. took political office.

Bishop's socialist ideology, according to the N.J.M., also contributed to the broadening of the island's economic base along other lines. The N.J.M. noted that Bishop embarked upon a policy of increasing the nation's import and export trade, promoting tourism, and developing the agricultural sector. He was also concerned with the building of new industries to package and process agricultural products and the building of new roads to facilitate transport.[11] Moreover, water, telephone, electricity and public transportation services were also upgraded. Perhaps the building of a 70 million dollar airport was Bishop's most significant achievement during his term in political office. It is alleged that whereas the Gairy regime spent a meager E.C. 8 million dollars on such national development in the period prior to the '79 revolution, the Bishop government, in comparison, spent roughly E.C. 237 million.[7]

Increased emphasis on the nation's economy,argued the N.J.M., was beneficial to the Grenadian masses at large. In the first place, unemployment which stood at 50 percent, prior to th> N.J.M. assuming political power, dropped to 10 percent - a decrease of 80 percent. Second, increased activity in the economic sector culminated in the stimulation of the nation's economy: it was responsible for a 10 pecent increase in the real wages of workers. Thirdly, an increase in both economic activity and worker wages resulted in a general increase in the standard of living.[10]

But Bishop's achievements were allegedly not limited to the economic sector. In education, too, he made great strides. Under Gairy, large numbers of children were not attending school and national functional illiteracy stood at 40 percent.[10] In addition, although under the law, primary education was compulsory from ages 5-16 years for both boys and girls, yet the law was never enforced. Young children were often "taken from school to care for younger siblings in order to allow mothers to work."[10] Also, very little or virtually no technical education was made available by the state. Although the Grenadian economy is primarily an agricultural one, agricultural science was rarely taught in schools and especially to girls.[10]

Under Bishop, a compulsory mass literacy, primary education, back to school campaign was started in September of 1980. This was accompanied by a mass adult education and new skills program that began in January of 1982. The N.J.M. claimed that Bishop's literacy campaign resulted in the reduction of illiteracy by 49 percent. And, a high proportion of both students and teachers in the campaign were women.[10] In August 1980, Bishop and the N.J.M. also created a special fund of U.S. $20,000 to assist low income mothers with the purchase of school books and uniforms. For the school year beginning in September 1981, the fund had increased and U.S. $75,000 in assistance had been given to the poorest of families.[10] They also instituted a school meals program which provided free milk to all pre-primary and primary school children and subsidized meals to more than half of all children in the nation.[10] Free secondary school education was also introduced in September 1981, and a school policy designed to teach technical subjects like metal work, domestic science, agricultural science and carpentry equally to boys and girls was also said to have been initiated.[10]

Under Gairy, sexual exploitation of women by government officials and private employers was highly prevalent. When Bishop came into power, claimed the P.R.G., consistent efforts were made to reverse the cycle of the exploitation of women and integrate them in the process of national development.[10] Thus, women were encouraged to play an increasingly important role in the national life of the island. For example, the number of women that were involved in active participation in their communities through membership in various community and mass organizations increased by 1,100 percent between March 1979 and September 1980. And the membership of the National Women's Organization (N.W.O.) doubled during 1981, reaching about 3,000 representing one out of every eight women.[10] In addition, legislation was adopted with the intent of curbing sexual harassment of women on the job, and they were assured equal pay for equal work. By virture of a newly adopted "maternity leave law" they were also to be given time off for childbirth with full or almost full pay.[12]

Bishop's achievements, it was reported, also expanded to other sectors of the nation's socio-economic and political infrastructure. In an interview with the New York Times, he said that he wanted to create in Grenada "a society that can provide the basic human needs - jobs, housing, health care, all the usual areas. To bring that about it must mean that you are going to have to develop a new political, cultural and economic dispensation for the country."[13]

Under Gairy, the public health system of Grenada was inadequate and in a state of total disarray. There were virtually no public health services. There were only a few doctors, and hospitals without medicine and equipment. National epidemics were also rampant. For example, in 1978, there were three national epidemics. In that same year the infant mortality rate was 29.5 per 1,000.[10] Under Bishop, the quality of medical services were said to have been improved. Medical care was made free, and a number of clinics were built throughout the nation. The number of health care personnel also increased significantly. Bishop also established a national insurance plan covering workers in both the public and private sectors and one that provided benefits such as sick pay, disability pay, pensions, retirement benefits, maternity leave pay, and monies to children of the deceased. He claimed that he exempted many workers from taxation and imposed taxes and fees of foreign-owned companies doing business in Grenada. Price controls on foreign foodstuffs were also imposed. Many poor families were granted interest free loans to make repairs to their homes and to build new ones. Some low interest loans were also made available to small farmers to assist them in agricultural pursuits. Finally, Bishop also instituted a land reform law which gave the P.R.G. the power to take over the developing of large plots of underutilized agricultural lands in an attempt to boost farming and agriculture, while at the same time, provide jobs for the nation's unemployed. [14]

From the data reported, it would seem that since the removal of Sir Eric Gairy from political office, Maurice Bishop and the N.J.M. somewhat succeeded in improving the quality of life of Grenadians through the input of national socialist policies. In the building of the revolution and in the improving of the quality of life, Grenada had poured money from "within". [14] The island had also received technical assistance from many socialist countries. Bishop had not only received financial aid from such socialist-oriented countries as Cuba, Libya, Nicaragua, North Korea, the Soviet Union, Syria, Vietnam, and several Eastern European bloc countries, but he also established strong diplomatic and trade relations and intense political ties with them. Bishop's identification with the socialist bloc reflects his ideological commitment. Not only did he hold dearly to the theoretical principles of scientific socialism but, as we have seen, he also committed himself to the realistic input of socialism into Grenadian society. For Bishop, the applicability of a revolutionary and socialist doctrine would not only reduce Black exploitation by the imperialists, but it would also break the stranglehold of capitalist elements and bring about true national liberation and equality of the Black masses, the majority of the nation's population, thus bringing about the socialist transformation he envisioned, and one that he had committed himself towards working to achieve. Meanwhile, he condemned the U.S. for refusing aid to the island and vowed that Grenada was a sovereign nation and "no longer in anybody's backyard." To him, the Grenadian struggle was "internationalist" in nature, and the island had joined the socialist bloc countries merely to collaborate with the liberation struggles of the world.

**Bishop's Failures:** While Bishop's ideology might have had a positive impact on a small segment of Grenadian society it, nevertheless, alienated the masses. This is clearly evident from certain events that occurred during the Prime Minister's term in political office.

Subsequent to his ascent to power, Bishop ruled with a dual

philosophy. On the one hand, he envisioned the socio-economic and political transformation of the condition of the Grenadian working class and, thus, the society as a whole, and allegedly committed himself to working towards that end. On the other hand, he committed a multiplicity of atrocities against the Grenadian people in the name of justice and in his attempt to maintain the form of political government he had opted for. Thus, a detailed discussion will serve to substantiate the validity of this allegation and to illustrate how Bishop's ideological and political philosophy and course of action culminated in alienating the masses of Grenadians from him and the P.R.G.

Writing in the Jamaican Daily Gleaner in early 1981, Vincent Tulloch noted that "Grenada should not have a third anniversary of the revolution."[14] Tulloch was addressing both the tyranny of the Bishop regime and heralding the launching of a campaign to oust the P.R.G. from the seat of political office because of the many atrocities it had committed. The P.R.G.'s new tyranny, as many have noted, was in many ways as harsh or even worse than that of the former dictatorship. Under P.R.G. rule there was brutality and curtailment of basic liberties in many areas.[15] Under Gairy, life in Grenada was said to be in the "frying pan". Under Bishop, it was said to be in the "fire" itself. Grenadians, according to an anonymous writer, had jumped "out of the frying pan into the fire."[16] The same writer proceeded to note that the Bishop regime that was set up on March 13 was misrepresented from the start and proved even more repressive than that of the ex-dictator Eric Gairy. "In his radio speech on the day of the coup, Bishop declared that a government would be formed from all elements opposed to Gairy. Elections would be held in the near future, all political parties would be free to hold meetings, the lives and property of expatriate residents would be safeguarded and those Grenadians who had suffered the acquisition of their land by the Gairy government would get it back or be given compensation. Till I left the island and so far as I know till now," this anonymous writer continued, "nobody has received compensation for acquired lands and none have been returned. No elections have been held, and it has been publicly announced, on the paltry excuse of a non-existent invasion attempt, that they have been postponed..."[16]

With Bishop in power, former allies and supporters of the P.R.G., as well as those opposed to it, were jailed and tortured. Many were also killed.[15] According to published reports, more than 350 people were arrested by Bishop in the weeks immediately following the revolution. While some were questioned and released yet, at the end of 1982, there were still around 75 political detainees held by the P.R.G.[17] In a New York Times article titled "Brooklyn Man Tells of Ordeal in Grenada Prison," it was noted that Bishop "kept an undertermined number of political opponents in prison" under inhumane conditions.[18] Anthony Langdon is a Grenadian citizen and a Permanent Alien Resident of the United States living in Brooklyn, New York. In 1979 he took a trip to Grenada to visit his ailing mother. While there, he was arrested by the Bishop regime and imprisoned for allegedly making remarks that were critical of the P.R.G. - a charge which he claims is unfounded. According to Langdon he was "kept with some 300 political prisoners at Richmond Hill Prison."[18] While there were never more than about 300 prisoners at this facility at any one time, yet the turnover was frequent. "Most people were arrested for about a nine-month term... They would let out about 100 and another 100 would come in... He estimated that during the four and a half years of the Bishop Government, as many as 6,000 Grenadians were detained at one time or another as political dissidents."[18]

While in prison, Mr. Langdon was also tortured by the Bishop regime. "Opening his shirt and displaying deep scars on his left side and chest," the interview continued, "Mr. Langdon said he had been shot at least three times with an AK-47 automatic rifle. . . They were putting me into the prison morgue when I began to cough up blood and they realized that I was alive... The doctors recommended that I be transferred to Barbados to have my lungs drained. . . but Maurice Bishop personally intervened and said I must not be allowed to leave the island. . . Mr. Langdon said he was often beaten but occasionally tortured."[18]

Similar events to the ones described by Anthony Langdon were intimated by Randolph Charles whose father was covertly killed by the P.R.G. In an exclusive interview with the leading newspaper of St. Vincent, The Vincentian, Randolph Charles said that "his father, Ralph Thompson, a one-time member of the P.R.G. became a victim of the revolution because he expressed dissatisfaction with certain brutalities. As a result of this he was kidnapped."[15] His father, he said, "died in jail on October 22, 1981, as a result of poisoning. After his father's death, he attempted to see the authorities but his request was refused."[19]

Bishop's repressive hand also extended to the domain of human rights. In keeping with the tradition of totalitarian regimes, he denied the Grenadian citizenry the execution of fundamental human rights. For example, the U.S., on many occasions, had seized the opportunity to raise allegations of what it regarded as blatant violations of human rights.[20]

Under Bishop, significant questions pertaining to human rights did not seem to apply: Grenada was a country where people lived under conditions of virtual bondage, where there were political prisoners who laid incarcerated in jails without the hope of ever receiving a fair trial. Despite Maurice Bishop's insistence that the human rights of "all detainees are protected and monitored by church-related regional institutions," yet a C.B.S. documentary cited proof of torture and repression of the Grenadian masses by the P.R.G.[21] In September, 1982, The Trinidad Express also attested to the violation of human rights. It reported, "The Inter-American Commission on Human Rights (I.A.C.H.R.) at the Organization of American States meeting has advised that the Grenada Government has been given the right to make an oral response to the petition filed against it. The petition complains of violations of human rights in Grenada contrary to the American Convention of Human Rights"[22] It is alleged that "the right of the people of Grenada to participate in Government has been violated. No elections have taken place since the March 13, 1979 coup that brought Prime Minister Maurice Bishop to power... A release issued by the petitioners noted that the closure of the Torchlight newspaper and the suspension of the Catholic Focus newspaper violates the right to freedom of thought and expression. Neither newspaper is now functional."[22] And while on a visit to New York, Maurice Bishop was questioned about his violation of human rights in that Caribbean island. His response seemed to confirm some of the allegations. According to the Amsterdam News, Bishop's attitude at this meeting was "totally one of 'welcomed revenge' rather than the 'brotherly love' he rantingly advocated for his enemies..."[23] Bishop also blasted a number of ad-hoc human rights committees and denounced his opposition back in Grenada. When asked about what he had done to his political opponents back home, his response was "What kind of bogus questioning is that?"[23] He proceeded to assure his New York audience that political opponents in Grenada were "fine and well and "under lock and key".[23]

Repression by Bishop and the P.R.G. was also quite visible within the media. The island's leading newspaper, The Torchlight, which at first supported the revolution, soon became exceedingly critical of it.[24] For this reason, Bishop, "who allegedly tolerated no opposition," found it most convenient to suppress the paper by closing it down in late 1979.[25] The same fate was also meeted out to The Grenadian Voice. Reports have indicated that Bishop not only banned this newspaper,[14] but he also had his security forces seize existing copies sold on newsstands and on the streets.[26] He then proceeded to "pass a new law preventing the publication of any newspaper on the island during the next year until a media policy is formulated."[27] As Bishop viewed it, "no further newspapers were to be published until a code of media policy" was issued by the government. A comprehensive media code was not completed up until the time of Bishop's death in October of 1983.[26]

Bishop's tyranny was also visibly dominant within other sectors of Grenadian life. For example, it is alleged that the P.R.G. seized property belonging to Grenadians without any compensation.[15] It harassed and prevented journalists from leaving the island to attend regional meetings.[15] It murdered suspected dissidents and detained "influential professionals, union leaders and teachers."[15] According to one report, Grenadians were "now suffering under the new dictatorship of Bishop."[15]

"The P.R.G. has also been repressive in its treatment of popular religious groups such as the Muslims and Rastafarians, two groups which ironically contributed actively to the rise of Bishop and the overthrow of Gairy."[15] Many Muslim leaders who supported Bishop in '79 were now in jail and many were killed in their beds by P.R.G. soldiers.[15] Traditional churches were harassed and both Anglican and Catholic bodies "searched, villified and labelled C.I.A. agents and counter-revolutionaries... The P.R.G.'s excesses have been condemned by Bishops of both churches. Bishop Drexel Gomez, head of the anglican church in Barbados has stated that 'the P.R.G. will probably continue to rule by the power of the gun and the bomb until a new order is born'."[15]

The inhumane attitude of the Bishop regime was also quite discernable by the way it treated workers and union officials. Many of these persons were intimidated and fled the island.[15] "Others such as Eric Pierre were detained. Kenneth Budhlall, head of the Trivoli Young Workers Cooperative (T.Y.W.C.)... is still in jail. Budhlall and his workers had been leading opponents of the ousted Gairy regime."[15] Cases like Budhlall's were not unique. They were clear indications of the "dishonest and inhuman nature of the P.R.G."[15] According to a published report, "if one wants to make an objective assessment of the actions and intentions of the P.R.G., the best place to begin it is by inquiring about the present status of the top former allies of Bishop, that is of those who helped him to get into power. It is a chain of horrors, of the P.R.G. murdering ex-officers in bed, of forced exile, of savage smear campaigns against influential grass roots figures or suspected dissidents.

It is a record of violence, intimidation, militaristic and totalitarian usurpation of the people's authority and a denial of the right of Grenadians to self determination."[15]

The impact of the P.R.G.'s repression of the Grenadian masses was accentuated by a shrinking economy and terrible socio-economic conditions. Under Bishop, Grenada went through a major recession which had a serious effect on the economy. For example, the island was importing almost all of its manufactured goods and producing virtually nothing. In 1979, Grenada earned a mere $56 million from its economic mainstays, bananas, cocoa and nutmeg, and spent $117 million on imports, thus leaving a $61 million deficit.[28] In 1980, Grenada's national earnings fell to $44 million because of a drop in world prices of "certain export items especially cocoa which fell from $12,000 to $6,000 per ton."[28] Meanwhile, import costs soared to $135 million which meant that there was a deficit of $91 million.[28]

The problem was aggravated by severe rainstorms, heavy flooding, and serious hurricane damage in late 1979 and early 1980. During this period, roughly 40 percent of the banana crop, 20 percent of cocoa, and 27 percent of nutmeg was destroyed because of these disasters. The estimated cost of this loss was approximately U.S. $20 million. "This was followed by a further blast of torrential rains in April 1981, when a further five million U.S. dollars damage was done."[29] According to Chris Searle, "these problems were compounded by an 8.8 percent reduction in stay-over visitors, thus hitting the tourist industry."[29] Morever, severe rainstorms had caused extensive damages and/or totally destroyed roads, bridges, schools, and social service facilities. The condition of the Grenadian masses was made doubly difficult by the existence of a 20 percent unemployment problem and a Gross Domestic Product (G.D.P.) per capita of below $600 (as to when compared with a G.D.P. per capita of $2,000 in neighbouring Barbados).[25] According to a New York Times report when "translated into human terms, these figures represent malnutrition, disease, high mortality, some of the Western Hemisphere's most wretched slums (electricity, running water, and sewers are often nonexistent), rampant crime - and, worst of all, little or no hope for a better future.[25] Many immigrants from Grenada emigrate to more prosperous nations like Barbados, Trinidad, Venezuela or the U.S.[25] "The present population of Grenada, which is roughly the size of Martha's Vineyard, is about 110,000 with about twice that number abroad. 'If all of them came back' a Grenadian official remarked recently, 'the island would simply sink'."[25]

That Grenada was allegedly economically weak soon became the subject of some discussion. In December 1982, George Bush, the United States Vice President, speaking at a Miami conference on Latin America and the Caribbean, noted that Grenada is an economically weak country and, as such, it was very much dependent.[29] Bush's allegations was subsequently rebutted by the P.R.G. In responding to the former's allegations, the latter charged that the U.S. Vice President's accusations were unfounded and cited a World Bank Report (W.B.R.) which indicated that Grenada was witnessing striking economic progress at a rate of 3 percent per annum.[29]

Despite the P.R.G.'s denial of Bush's charges, it appears that there was some legitimacy to what the latter had to say. Bush's claim was made apparent by the fact that during the period 1980-81, Grenada made several attempts to procure loans and bilateral assistance from the United States, requests which were repeatedly rejected. The island also sought economic assistance from the Organization of American States Emergency Unit (O.A.S.E.U.) and from the E.E.C. Some assistance was later received from these bodies.

Grenada's economic "hard-times" and the P.R.G.'s lack of available monies, coupled with Bishop's bloody and repressive hand, soon impacted on the local masses. During the period 1979 to 1983, the duration of political rule by the P.R.G., labor disturbances and a wave of strikes erupted throughout the nation. In late 1979, workers at the Grenada Electricity Company (GRENLEC) threatened to go on a national strike if certain demands of their's were not met by the P.R.G. So too in late 1980, the Seamen and Waterfront Workers Union (S.W.W.U.) refused to unload a cargo of milk that had been donated to Grenada from certain European countries.

Expressions and gestures of worker dissatisfaction with the P.R.G. were also made abundantly clear by certain events that occurred in early 1981. GRENLEC and the nation's Public Workers Union (P.W.U.) collaborated to create widespread labor disturbances throughout the country; they were protesting against the P.R.G.'s refusal to accomodate their demand for pay increases. And in mid-1981, two multinational companies operating in Grenada, Barclays Bank and Esso, also exposed the P.R.G.'s request for a loan, and Esso, too, threatened to cut off oil supply if the P.R.G. did not settle its debts immediately. Finally, in early

1982, three of Grenada's leading labor unions voiced their opposition to the P.R.G. The Grenada Union of Teachers (G.U.T.), the P.W.U., and the Technical and Allied Workers Union (T.A.W.U.) refused to report to work during the course of labor negotiations with the P.R.G. These unions were protesting against the P.R.G.'s repressive hand as well as its refusal to accomodate their request for pay increases. Of course, such action had disastrous effects on the Grenadian economy.

Workers dissatisfaction with the P.R.G., coupled with the latter's inability to move the country ahead socio-economically, also soon led to widespread counter-revolutionary activities.[28] Immediately following the revolution, the National Youth Organization (N.Y.O.), which had earlier supported Bishop in ousting Gairy from the seat of political office, became disenchanted with the former and began addressing such problems as unemployment, education, housing, health, and inadequate recreational, sporting and cultural facilities.[30] Not only was this organization able to cite the bankruptcy of the Bishop regime, but it also began organizing in an attempt to drive it from political office.

Counter-revolutionary activity as a means of expressing dissatisfaction with the Bishop regime was also amply demonstrated throughout Bishop's term in political office. For example, around mid-1979, a wave of arson swept through Grenada with much of it directed towards governmental agencies. Later that same year, a police corporal named Wilton de Raveniere, and a supporter of Gairy named Winston Whyte, admitted to plotting to overthrow the Bishop regime. Then in the Spring of 1980, the Budhlall Gang, controlled by brothers Kenneth and Russell Budhlall, began organizing large sections of Rastafarians and the nation's youth in an attempt to assassinate P.R.G. leaders and, thus, overthrow the existing political regime. [31] The plan was eventually uncovered and the Budhlalls, as well as those involved in the plot, were subsequently arrested and imprisoned.[31] Similarly, on June 19, 1980 at a Heroes Day rally in Queens Park, St. George's, a powerful time-bomb was effectively detonated close to Maurice Bishop's seat. The blast missed its intended target, Maurice Bishop. It did, however, kill a few people and injure dozens of others. Also, in mid-1980, Stanley Cyrus and James Herry, two alleged counter-revolutionaries, also stepped up their activities against the Bishop regime. Cyrus, a Grenadian, teaching at Howard University in the U.S., was named as the key figure in a plot designed to crush the P.R.G. by assassinating Bishop and other heads of his political machinery.[32] And Herry was publicly exposed for collecting large quantities of arms and ammunition and passing them on to counter-revolutionaries in the Mount Rich area in an attempt to over-throw Bishop.[32] Early in June 1980, Glen Simon and Habib Ali, two anti-Bishop terrorists, attacked and seriously wounded a number of the P.R.G.'s militiamen.[32] Later that year, on November 17, 1980, Simon and Ali attacked a car with four P.R.G. sympathizers and killed a militiaman who was then on duty.[32] Finally, in mid-1981, one Michael Perdue, a sympathizer of the Gairy regime, was arrested for being in collusion with ex-dictator Gairy and for plotting the violent overthrow of Bishop.

Certainly counter-revolutionary activity during the P.R.G.'s rule was rampant; it was a clear indication that Bishop's popularity was waning. Although the N.J.M. leader was earlier seen as the "New Messiah" that would utlimately deliver the Grenadian masses from the pangs of socio-economic and political repression, he too, just like ex-dictator Gairy, soon reached the point of unpopularity. The people who had worked alongside and supported him were now disenchanted with his poor showing. It could be argued that Grenadians themselves were unhappy about the revolution as well as the inability of Bishop to progressively develop the nation. Grenadians quickly began realizing that slogans, speeches, rallies, and mere political rhetoric on the part of the P.R.G., were simply not enough in the pursuit of development. The fact was that Grenada was a poor nation; it simply did not have money to develop internally. Thus, the ideology that Bishop had embarked upon could not solve the island's problems. While Bishop's concern for Black Power might well have been noble, yet rhetoric and slogans were simply not going to deliver his people. Compounding this problem was that Bishop pursued an anti-capitalist and an anti-imperialist course of action which meant that there was a de-emphasis on both capitalist elements and a capitalist mode of production. This situation served as a deterrent to internal national development. Finally, Bishop's embarkation on a revolutionary and socialist course of action transformed Grenada into a totalitarian state. Rule by the "Bullet" rather than by the "Buck" and "Bible" was a way of life Grenadians - a plantation oriented society people - were not used to. Furthermore, in the pursuit of accomplishing his revolutionary and socialist ideals, Bishop ruled with an "iron fist"; he repressed and suppressed the Grenada citizenry in an attempt to perpetuate the interests of the P.R.G., irrespective of the aspirations of the local citizenry. While Bishop did make some modest gains on account of the pursued ideology, his failures seemed to have outweighed his accomplishments. He alienated the Grenadian citizenry and soon became unpopular; he was, therefore, the target of much counter-revolutionary activity.

A brief examination of some of the issues caught up in Bishop's successes and failures might also shed some light on this problem. A quick review of the relevant literature indicates that, as far as the alleged successes of Bishop were concerned, most of the reporting was done by the P.R.G.'s press. Let us recall that once Bishop assumed political power, he closed down the national press. This meant that the P.R.G.'s press, now the main news disseminating body in the country, was free to report anything it wanted. Given this situation, therefore, the reporting of news by the P.R.G.'s press was confined largely to depicting favorable things about the revolution. In addition, most of what was reported was mere propaganda and not actual achievements. If one accepts the reported successes of Bishop, one would be puzzled as to why he eventually became unpopular. In other words, if what Bishop said about his achievements was true, then why did Grenadians get to the point where they rejected him and were engaged in counter-revolutionary activities in an attempt to depose him? While recognizing that Bishop did make some modest gains, most of what was reported, however, was propaganda-oriented, according to Grenadians we interviewed. This attests to the P.R.G.'s elaborate propaganda machinery and lends support to the ultimate disenchantment of the Grenadian masses with that political organization. Grenadian disillusionment with the P.R.G. was prompted by the course of action the latter embarked upon. If the success the P.R.G. claimed was true then it might be reasonable to ask, why did the condition of the Grenadian working class remain virtually unchanged? In the authors' interviews with Grenadians, they indicated that their socio-economic and political condition under Bishop was no better than it was under Gairy. Most claimed that if changes were being made for the better, as Bishop claimed, they were not seeing them. In fact, most noted that it was worse under Bishop than under Gairy, despite the P.R.G.'s allegations to the contrary. Many Grenadians pointed out that the transportation, health, hospital, water, electricity, traffic, road and other systems pertaining to vital social services were worse in 1983 than they were in 1979 when Bishop assumed political power.

Grenadian assessment of the situation is, after all, true. There is overwhelming support for their position. Since the P.R.G. came into power, there was a marked deterioration of vital social services on the island: the P.R.G. simply did not have money to upgrade them. This was aggravated by a shrinking economy and a severe economic crisis. Although the P.R.G. did receive some monies from socialist-bloc countries, it was by far not enough to alleviate the island's economic troubles. Given the lack of available monies, how could Bishop claim the huge successes we alluded to earlier in this chapter? The answer is clear. The P.R.G. sought to deceive the Grenadian masses by reporting that the revolution was successful when in fact, it was encountering difficulties on most fronts. Suffice to say that it did not take long for Grenadians to discover this and, when they did, it was one of the primary sources of their discontent. Of course, this was aggravated by the secret nature of the P.R.G.'s operations and the repressive hand with which it ruled. What did all of this mean to Grenadians? It meant that the P.R.G., despite its claims, could boast little of its achievements: its failures and public deceptions were perhaps more pronounced, and these were reasons enough to antagonize and alienate Grenadians from both the P.R.G. and its principal leaders.

As we will observe in the section that follows, Grenadian disenchantment not only resided with Bishop by 1983, but also with other leaders of the N.J.M., particularly with Deputy Prime Minister Bernard Coard. But who was Coard and what was his ideological preoccupation? Was Coard's ideology different from that of Bishop's? And to what extent did Coard and his ideology, as well as the course of action he embarked upon, aid or alter the success of the revolution?

## Bernard Coard: The Man and His Ideology

Bernard Coard, the son of middle class parents, was born in St. George's on August 10, 1944. He attended Palmer Public Elementary School and the Grenada Boy's Secondary School. In the early sixties he left Grenada to study Economics and Political Science at Brandeis University in the U.S. He graduated from that institution in 1966. Coard received the M.A. in Comparative Political Economy from Sussex University, England, in 1967. Upon receiving the M.A., he enrolled in the Ph.D. program at Sussex. His research interest was Latin America.

While in England, Coard worked in community development and also taught school for two years. In the early seventies, he returned to the Caribbean where, until 1974, he was a lecturer at the University of the West Indies at St. Augustine, Trinidad. From 1974-76 he was a member of the Department of Management Studies and Government at the Mona campus of the University in Jamaica. Coard is married and has two children. His wife, Phyllis, is an educator and was Deputy Minister of Women's Affairs in Bishop's government.

After the 1979 revolution, Coard, a long time associate of Bishop's, was asked to return to Grenada to become Minister of Finance of the P.R.G. But once in Grenada, Coard's inability to get along with Bishop led to a situation of open confrontation with the latter. A review of Coard's ideological outlook reveals that it was somewhat strikingly similar to that of Bishop's in that both men rantingly advocated Black Power, revolution, anti-imperialism and anti-capitalism, Marxism-Leninism, and scientific socialism. Since we have already outlined the central elements of each of these concerns, we will not attempt to reiterate them here.

Given the similarity of Bishop's and Coard's ideology, one must ask: what is it that led to the confrontation between the two men? As we will demonstrate, the confrontation can be viewed primarily in terms of commitment to ideological intensity, the approach opted for by each man, the existence of a situation of personal hate and family squabbles, and Coard's secrecy. Although both Coard and Bishop followed a Marxist-Leninist path, yet Bishop advocated a soft-line approach whereas Coard opted for a more orthodox one. Coard, on several occasions, criticized Bishop for "allowing private enterprise to participate in rebuilding the economy."[33] He was also critical of Bishop's decision to have a special commission write a new constitution in preparation for elections scheduled for 1985. Instead of open and free elections, Coard advocated zonal councils and people's committees. He used his influence on the Central Committee to get some of his ideas and programs adopted. Coard also controlled a semi-secret group known as the Organization for Educational Advancement and Research (O.E.A.R.).[34] This organization was founded in the early 1970's and functioned as a clique within the N.J.M. or as a party within a party.

The rivalry between Bishop and Coard deepened as the revolution progressed. On October 14, 1983, to dispel rumors that he was involved in a plot to assassinate Maurice Bishop, Coard resigned. It was widely believed that the latter was instrumental in the October 19, killing of Bishop and a number of governmental Ministers. He was a key figure in the military coup that followed and played a major role in the R.M.C. that ruled Grenada for a few days. Coard, along with the other members of the R.M.C., was captured by U.S. military personnel subsequent to its intervention on the island. Since his capture, he has been held at the Richmond Hill prison where he is awaiting trial.

We noted earlier that perhaps one of the more important reasons why the Grenada revolution failed was because of its destruction from within.

In other words, the revolution failed because of the actions of leaders within the ranks of the N.J.M., particularly Bernard Coard. Let us recall that Coard, very much unlike Bishop, was a hard-line Marxist. He was unhappy with Bishop for not socializing the country faster, and for being unwilling to engage in a process of "collective leadership".[35] Such a difference in belief meant that, sometime following the revolution, Coard had parted company with Bishop. Subtle ideological differences had indeed created a split between the two men, and this later spilled over into a situation of personal hate and vengeance.

Aggravating the situation between the two men was the relationship that existed between their wives, Angela Bishop and Phyllis Coard. Phyllis, a seasoned politician and staunch supporter of the Marxist-Leninist ideology, assisted her husband and other members of the Central Committee in formulating programs and in developing policy decisions for the P.R.G. In other words, she was actively involved in the day to day running of Grenada. Angela, on the other hand left the politics of Grenada to her husband and instead was more concerned with the welfare and happiness of Maurice and her children. This outsider role enabled Angela to see things about the P.R.G. that Maurice failed to see. It is common knowledge in Grenada that Angela told her husband on several occasions that he should keep a closer watch on Bernard and Phyllis. She warned the Prime Minster that he should pay more attention to the Central Committee and to the army. From what we can ascertain, Bishop did not pay much attention to his wife's advice. In frustration, Angela and her children left and migrated to Canada.

An informant and close associate and neighbor of both Phyllis and Angela, who themselves were next door neighbors, told the authors that both women hated each other. On several occasions, we were told, "they openly 'fussed' at one another and even exchanged a couple of blows on one occasion." From this it might be reasonable to assume that the differences in ideology, social outlook, and dislike for one another that existed between Phyllis and Angela helped to aggravate the already strained relationship that existed between Bishop and Coard.

Although personal hate and vengeance was important, it was not the only variable responsible for straining the relationship that existed between Bishop and Coard. Some other factors were also crucial. Since around mid-1982, Coard began forming his own clique within the ranks of the N.J.M. He surrounded himself with top party members who allegedly shared his political views and opposed those of Maurice

Bishop. This situation not only exacerbated the split between the two men, but it also clearly exposed the fact that the N.J.M. was split into two separate and distinct political factions. Since its formation, Coard's clique functioned as a factional and secret group within the N.J.M.

Subsequent to the ideological parting of both men, Coard made a desperate bid for power. His main tactical weapon was to use both fact and slander against Maurice Bishop in an attempt to unseat him. According to the Deputy Prime Minister, Bishop was the main cause of the difficulties of the revolution. As he put it, "Maurice was the real problem"; therefore, he had to be removed from political office.

Coard explained to his factional grouping that he was both dissatisfied and disenchanted with the pace of change in Grenada. He noted that the transformation from democracy to socialism was not taking place fast enough, and it was Bishop who should be blamed for this. Coard opted for and argued in favor of a more rapid transformation to socialism. As he envisioned it, Grenada's internal socio-economic and political development could only be effectively realized with a rigid and swift input of socialist principles and political doctrines of Marxism-Leninism. To him, Maurice Bishop was not intensely committed to these ideals, nor was he capable of making political judgements in the direction of positive changes based on these ideals. In fact, Coard viewed Bishop as the main cause of the country's socio-economic problems.

Coard's hatred for Bishop, coupled with his intent to drive the latter from political office, was made manifest in the nature of the campaign which he waged against the Prime Minister. Being a key member of the Central Committee of the P.R.G., Coard used much deceit, cunning, and propaganda to persuade other N.J.M. leaders that Bishop lacked socialist skills and strategy. Coard noted that Bishop was incompetent as both party leader and Prime Minister and would thus be ineffective as the key political figure responsible for national socio-economic development and eventual societal transformation to socialism.

Through his cunning tactics, Coard had little difficulty finding an audience receptive to his ideas. While some of his support came from the civilian arm of the P.R.G., a significant amount of it, however, also came from the military; that is, from top-ranking officers of the P.R.A. who were also members of the Central Committee. Such personalities as Governmental Minister of Mobilization, Selwyn Stratchan and ranking military officers General Hudson Austin, Major Leon Cornwall, Major Liam James, and Major Ewart Layne were most sympathetic to Coard's ideas. Coard's wife Phyllis, head of the N.W.O. and a key member of the Central Committee, was also part of the group.[34]

Finding an audience for his ideas was important to Coard for a number of reasons. In the first place, support for his ideas would give leverage to his argument against Maurice Bishop. Second it would expose the weaknesses of Bishop and might even turn party members against him. Third, Coard would be able to consolidate a power base, a vital and necessary ingredient if he was to oust Maurice Bishop from the seat of political office and, thus, take power himself.

Coard used the consolidation of this power base to his fullest advantage, especially in his bid for power. In a September 1983 meeting of the Central Committee, one of Coard's supporters, Major Liam James, acting on covert orders from Coard, "placed a motion on the floor calling for Bishop to relinquish part of his leadership responsibilities to Coard. Bishop was to handle mass work and international relations... Bernard Coard was to take over internal party work and overall strategy."[7] When the vote on this issue was later taken, the Central Committee had acted and Bishop, whether willing or not, was to relinquish part of his perogatives as the leader of the P.R.G. In other words, Bishop was now to share the leadership role of the P.R.G. with Bernard Coard.

According to published reports, Bishop welcomed the Central Committee's decision. He was not opposed to the idea of sharing the leadership role with Bernard Coard.[36] If anything, he was willing to accomodate both Coard and the decision reached by the Central Committee.

However, Bishop had some difficulty understanding the particulars of the decision. In his view of things, the joint leadership proposal was not designed to give equal power with Coard. Instead, it was merely a scheme aimed at systematically stripping Bishop of his power and control within the ranks of the party. Meanwhile, it would give Bernard Coard increasing power thus creating a situation of "power imbalance" between the two leaders. With Coard having more power than Bishop, it would be relatively simple for the former to implement rigid socialist principles and run the P.R.G. along orthodox Marxist-Leninist lines.[36] It would mean the ultimate weakening of Bishop's position. Thus, given the complications implied by the decision rendered by the Central Committee that Bishop share power with Coard, Bishop requested that he be given time to think about the "practical applications" of this decision which he did not understand, as well as what it might mean in terms of its wider implications for both him and the party as a whole.

At the end of September 1983, while Bishop was allegedly still in the process of thinking over the Central Committee's decision, he took a trip abroad to tend to governmental business. While away, Coard, now the acting Prime Minister of the island, seized the opportunity to strengthen and thus secure his own position. He waged a vicious campaign against Bishop and used his customary slander and deceit in an attempt to unseat the absent Prime Minister.

Coard also trumped up a number of charges against Bishop. For example, he accused the latter of being a dictator and unwilling to share power. Coard also noted that Bishop was an "opportunist" who was not following party guidelines; that he was a "dangerous individual", and should be expelled from the party. Most vicious of all, Coard charged that Bishop was spreading a rumor that he (Coard) was plotting to assassinate him (Bishop).

On September 8, 1983, Bishop returned from his trip abroad. He proceeded to request a meeting of the Central Committee to discuss the joint leadership proposal. When the Central Committee met, Bishop was the prime target of opposition and criticism. Coard and his faction confronted the Prime Minister with each of the alleged charges and proceeded to condemn him. Towards the end of the meeting, the Central Committee, now strongly influenced and controlled by Coard and in total condemnation of Bishop, voted to place Bishop under "House Arrest".

From October 13 to October 19, 1983, a period of roughly one week, Maurice Bishop was under "House Arrest". Then on the morning of October 19, 1983, two of Bishop's governmental ministers, Fitzroy Bain and Unison Whiteman, led a demonstration of about 4,000 to 5,000 people who successfully freed Bishop. With Bishop leading the way, the demonstrators subsequently marched to Fort Rupert, the Army headquarters. Immediately following their arrival at the Fort, Bernard Coard, who at this point seemed to have the support of the Army, quickly summoned three armored personnel carriers.

Then suddenly it was pandemonium. These armored vehicles began firing a barrage of bullets and automatic weapons into the crowd. Many of the demonstrators were killed and scores of others wounded. Realizing that many more lives could be lost, if something was not done quickly, Maurice Bishop and a few other governmental ministers involved in this demonstration quickly surrendered. According to reports, they were taken inside Fort Rupert and murdered by Coard's men.

Who ordered these murders? The consensus of opinion among Grenadians is that it was Bernard Coard. From the turn of events, it is perhaps not difficult to believe this. All indications are that it was Coard who was, in fact, the main culprit.[37] Coard had indeed betrayed Maurice Bishop and, with a successful U.S. invasion of the island following the short-lived R.M.C., which was established subsequent to the assassination of Bishop, he might well have been instrumental in betraying the revolution itself. Truly, Coard's action might have been responsible for Washington's success, and might have well been the key factor responsible for the demise and failure of this once popular revolution in Grenada.

# CHAPTER FIVE

# LEADERSHIP IN
# THE GRENADA REVOLUTION

## Introduction

In this chapter, we will examine the ideas and actions of the leadership of the Grenada revolution and note their impact on the outcome of the revolution. An attempt will be made to show that the ideas and actions of the leadership were both contrary to the aspirations and expectations of the Grenadian citizenry and, thus, not conducive to that society. Consequently, they were not popular in character and assisted in contributing to the revolution's failure. The leadership's many shortcomings and oversights regarding certain crucial issues in the revolution also contributed to its demise.

The ideas and actions of the leadership of revolutions are important factors in determining their eventual outcomes., Ideas and actions can determine how the national populace comes to view a revolution, and the degree to which they identify with it., Therefore, who the revolutionary leaders are, their ideological preoccupations, the interests and aspirations they represent, the image they project to the national populace, and their methods of organization, are some of the factors that can serve either to inhibit or enhance national societal identification with and acceptability of their cause. Thus, it might be argued that the success or failure of a revolution is largely dependent upon people's perception of the leadership and the course of action it pursues.,

The analysis of the ideas and actions of the leadership of the Grenada revolution, particularly those of the principal leaders, Maurice Bishop, Bernard Coard, and Unison Whiteman, will be examined within the context of three specific time frames.

The first begins in early 1973 when M.A.P. and J.E.W.E.L. merged to form the N.J.M., and extends to March 12, 1979, the day immediately before the overthrow of Gairy. During this period, repression and political corruption by the Gairy regime, as well as existent foreign exploitation and metropolitan domination of the society, were key concerns of the N.J.M., the vanguard revolutionary organization. The N.J.M. leadership also formulated an all-inclusive ideology that most of the national Black working class were able to identify with. This identification was important to the leadership's mobilization efforts, particularly the degree to which the masses committed themselves to the ideology and to the emergent leadership of the N.J.M. on the whole. Leadership's main thrust during this period had been toward the mobilization of dissenting urban and rural working class forces: it had, therefore, not confined its activities largely to particular geographical and ecological niches within Grenadian society. In addition, leadership's involvement in community issues and working class struggles that involved both the urban and rural elements of the population demonstrated its ability initially to establish links of communication and bases of popular support within these communities and, thus, bring members of the national working class under its hegemony.

The second period began with the overthrow of Eric Gairy on March 13, 1979, and extended to October 12, 1983, the day immediately before the house arrest of Maurice Bishop. The popularity and degree of success the N.J.M. leadership enjoyed in the first period, was not to be accorded it in the second. During this period, leadership's inability to fulfill the expectations of the masses coupled with its reneging of promises were essentially responsible for the public's negative perception and non-acceptance of it. Its repressive hand and intense degree of secrecy were also crucial to the process. The false and misleading image of the revolution that leadership presented to the public, and its concern for the transformation of a colonial and plantation oriented society to a military state, were also key issues to contend with.

The third and final period began on October 13, 1983, with the house arrest of Maurice Bishop and extended to October 25, 1983, the day the United States invaded Grenada. During this period, the political split and internal power struggle between Maurice Bishop and Bernard Coard came to a climax. Because of existing ideological differences and an alleged disloyalty to party mandates, Bishop was placed under house arrest and subsequently assassinated by Coard's faction of the N.J.M. This action not only paved the way for the ousting of Bishop's faction of the N.J.M. from political power, but it also set the stage for the manufacturing of the military coup that followed, one that was allegedly covertly masterminded by Coard himself. The period also witnessed widespread internal political chaos. Also, the U.S. invaded this tiny Caribbean island and overthrew the newly established ruling military junta that had so ruthlessly seized power a few days earlier. Not having a designated second line of leadership to continue the struggle against the invading forces, that is in the period subsequent to the capturing and imprisonment of the key leaders of the revolution, the ruling military junta quickly folded under the armed military might of the U.S.

## Time Frame One: Early 1973 to March 13, 1979

As we noted earlier, the N.J.M. was formed in March of 1973 through the merging of two organizations, J.E.W.E.L. and M.A.P.₂ This organization initially emerged with the intention of addressing the socioeconomic and political repression of the Grenadians by the Gairy regime and, thus, making known its affirmation to drive Gairy from the seat of political office, and to come and take power itself.

Although the N.J.M.'s primary concern was to alleviate the oppressed condition of the Grenadian masses by driving the dictator Eric Gairy from political office, the organization did not confine itself solely to that issue. Its emergent leadership quickly began to question metropolitan domination and foreign capitalist exploitation of the society. The N.J.M.'s concern was to break the stranglehold White foreign capitalist elements had on the socio-economic and political reins of the country, thus stripping them of the absolute control they had within these sectors of the social system.

The N.J.M. leadership envisioned a transferring of power and control from the hands of White foreign capitalists to the Black element of the population, the majority of Grenada's population. Also it advocated that Blacks be made masters of their own destinies, hence the slogan "Black Power". The N.J.M. contemplated a total societal change through the revolutionary process and the input of a system of true equality based on socialist doctrines. Thus, what had started as merely the local concern for the removal of Eric Gairy from political office was quickly transformed into an issue of international ramifications, and one that was oriented towards a radical and total transformation of the society.

What precipitated this concern for a transformation? Gairy's politically corrupt ways and his repression of the Grenadian masses, and the fact that he was in collusion with White foreign capitalists, forced the N.J.M. leadership to focus attention not only on Gairy but also on foreign elements that had aligned themselves with him. Gairy, according to the N.J.M., was a "lackey of imperialism" who, since the days of plantation society in Grenada, had been serving and perpetuating the interests of the White foreign metropole at the expense of locally oppressed peoples. An understanding of Gairy's politics and actions, therefore, would have only been piecemeal in terms of the N.J.M.'s accurately assessing the Grenada situation. What was also needed, as the N.J.M. leadership saw it, was an analysis of White metropolitan interests as they operated on the island and the degree to which Gairy was subservient to them. According to the N.J.M., both of these factors had to be explored in order to arrive at a comprehensive picture of the Grenada situation.

Subsequent to its formation, the N.J.M. toured the entire island drumming up support for its cause.₃ It denounced both the Gairy regime and the foreign multinationals operating in the country, and advocated sweeping revolutionary changes for the society. Prior to the emergence of the N.J.M. on the Grenadian political scene, the persistence of economic problems, attributed primarily to the Gairy regime and the multinationals, was responsible for widespread unemployment throughout the nation and had culminated in the formation of many organizations and groups.₃ Because of their disenchantment with Gairy and the domination of the local economy by metropolitan interests, the primary objective of most of these organizations and groups was the socio-economic advancement of the relative position they occupied in the society.₁ Also disenchanted with the existing state of economic affairs at the time were the masses of the unemployed and many sections of labor unions that had earlier supported Gairy.

The birth of the N.J.M. marked the national merging of these different factions and gave rise to a broad, but yet tightly-knit social movement. Despite the rural and urban collectivity of individuals, groups, and organizations, the N.J.M. became the vanguard revolutionary organization in the mobilization of forces.

The character of the N.J.M., endorsed and projected by the leadership during this period, was central to its activities. Since the formation of the N.J.M., the leadership's central concern was with the mobilization and consolidation of forces within the entire country. Prior to the merging of M.A.P. and J.E.W.E.L., M.A.P., under the leadership of Maurice Bishop, had worked mainly in the urban centers while J.E.W.E.L., led by Unison Whiteman, had concentrated its efforts primarily in the rural areas. This action on the part of leadership meant that it had in effect partitioned the island in an attempt to be more autonomous.

At the same time, it would have more control in different parts of the country and, thus, bring disenchanted individuals and groups under its control and influence. It also meant that the leadership had not only directed its efforts at an urban industrial working class section of the national population, but also at the enclaves of the rurally based working class. This fact clearly indicates that the leadership had not ignored the concerns of the working class. The partitioning of the island into both rural and urban sections, and the concentration of its efforts in both these geographic and ecological niches reveals the ulterior motive of the leadership of this organization: it reflects a genuine concern for the condition of the working class from a truly national perspective. Class was used as the binding variable irrespective of other existing differences. Despite residential segregation, the leadership was responsible for national solidarity, and this factor was not overlooked or dismissed too perfunctorily. It should be noted that residential segregation could have contributed to the lack of working class common understanding and identification with the N.J.M., as well as with its emergent leadership, but it did not because of the leadership's actions. Thus, the N.J.M.'s leadership had initially considered the consequences of residential segregation in terms of a crude summation of forces, and had acted in such a way so as to insure that it did not deter their concern for a national working class alliance.

It was during this period that the N.J.M.'s leadership formulated the ideological position of the organization. Since we have already discussed this ideology in some detail, we will merely reiterate the main ideas here. It is important to note that ideology was formulated around the interests and aspirations as well as the common socio-economic positon of both rural and urban working class Blacks. The belief in and emphasis on "Black Power" served as the binding ingredient for the Black working class, the majority of the national population. In addition, the throwing off of imperialist domination of Black people, the assumption of power through the Black revolutionary struggle, and the input of a socialist economic mode, all of which were central to the N.J.M.'s ideological preoccupation, also gave working class Blacks a sense of identification with the leadership and the struggle it was actively waging. The N.J.M.

had formulated an all-inclusive ideology that had taken into consideration the interests and aspirations of a disenchanted national working class: it had clearly succumbed to the demands of the people in an attempt to create an intense degree of cohesiveness and singleness of purpose, and had used such an ideology as a strategical and tactical weapon to identify with the masses of the working class and bring them under its control. An all-inclusive ideology, therefore, culminated in the non-alienation of large segments of the working class who, with a different ideology, might have virtually abstained from identification with and participation alongside the leadership of the N.J.M. in its bid to overthrow Gairy and assume the political reins of the country.

In the period prior to the overthrow of Gairy, the N.J.M.'s leadership was involved in community action and national struggles that involved the working class. During that period, the N.J.M. was the vanguard revolutionary political organization that posed a serious threat to the Gairy regime. Not only had it supported various groups and organizations opposed to Gairy, but it also organized protests, demonstrations and strikes, and actively participated in many. In early 1973, for example, the N.J.M. and its emergent leadership was instrumental in helping to organize electricity, telephone, and water workers who subsequently called a strike in April of that year. Later the same year, when the Gairy police brutally murdered a young man, Jerimiah Richardson, the N.J.M.'s leadership summoned for protest activities that ultimately created national chaos. In June of 1973, the N.J.M. called for a people's convention to denounce Gairy. More than 10,000 people attended. And in November of the same year, the N.J.M.'s leadership called a People's Congress where Gairy was tried and found guilty of committing twenty-seven crimes against the people of Grenada.

Realizing that the N.J.M. was becoming firmly entrenched as the political opposition in the island, and one that was beginning to pose a serious threat to his regime, Gairy responded with a show of desperation and defiance. He arrested both Maurice Bishop and Unison Whiteman. The two N.J.M. leaders were later brutally beaten and imprisoned.

But the N.J.M.'s leadership refused to yield to Gairy's oppression and overt violence. Immediately following their release from jail the organization's leadership, along with the "Committee of 22", which we referred to earlier, called for a national general strike. This strike which lasted for nearly three months, almost crippled the island.

In 1976 the N.J.M., still growing in popularity, felt strong enough to challenge the Gairy regime at the polls. It contested the national general elections held that year and won a number of political seats. Now officially recognized as the chief opposition party in the island, the N.J.M.'s leadership proceeded to use its newly acquired parliamentary position to denounce Gairy, and give leverage and legitimacy to its arguments.

From 1976 to 1979, the N.J.M.'s leadership continued its struggle which included demonstrations, protest activities and active involvement in labor disputes and strikes, all along the way drumming up support for its cause. Then in 1979, through the revolutionary process and armed insurgence, the N.J.M. forcefully ousted Eric Gairy from the seat of political office and assumed the political reins of the country.

The N.J.M.'s leadership involvement in community issues and national struggles conditioned working class acceptance of, identification with, and allegiance to it. Members of the national Black working class were able to identify with and relate to the N.J.M. and its emergent leadership. Identification with this political organization and its leaders was apparently facilitated by the commonalities of class, and by both the working class and the N.J.M.'s opposition to the Gairy regime. Class position, particularly on the part of the urban and rural masses, was the medium of identification and affiliation with the N.J.M.'s leadership. Class was also the binding ingredient for the N.J.M. and those who constituted the lower class. Thus, class is an important feature in societies like Grenada. Class position can provide a tangible set of common identifications, and can sometimes serve as the key element in situations of class allegiance. Class position also provides a legitimate identity for one, and may well carry over into situations of group affiliation and attachment.

The N.J.M.'s leadership involvement in community issues and national struggles which was primarily responsible for working class identification and affiliation with this revolutionary organization and its leadership, points to its ability to develop organs of popular support with the urban and rural Black communities. The leadership had, from the very beginning, sought to establish the N.J.M. as a viable revolutionary organization in wider Grenadian society, and one that was seriously committed to addressing the concerns of the masses of the working class. Its involvement in the wider society, therefore, was not ad-hoc or superficial in outlook, but it reflected a certain commitment to establish firm roots in every part of the island and thus not ignore or overlook opportunities to become identifiable with the mass of the working class population and engage them in active support. The N.J.M. leadership's ability to develop organs of popular support and actively engage the masses was vital in terms of the popularity it initially enjoyed. It was also essential to the downfall of Gairy and to the institution of the N.J.M. as the new political government of the country.

## Time Frame Two: March 13, 1979 to October 12, 1979

Prior to the overthrow of dictator Eric Gairy, the N.J.M.'s leadership had the popular support of the Grenada citizenry, particularly that of the working class. The revolution initially appealed to this strata of the national population. It appeared to be attractive and, for this reason, the people were willing to embrace and support it as well as the N.J.M.'s leadership that had successfully created it.

But the popularity of the N.J.M.'s leadership was shortlived. Immediately following the overthrow of Gairy, Bishop promised to alleviate the oppressed condition of the Grenadian masses but did relatively little towards achieving this goal. The condition of the Grenadian working class remained unchanged. His promise that the revolution would bring food and better social services in the country was more myth than reality.

Immediately following the installation of the N.J.M.'s political leadership into power, Grenada was hit with a serious national economic crisis. Bishop had inherited from the Gairy regime an economy that was in a state of total disarray. It was also a time when the Grenadian national economy was shrinking. What were the implications of this? While the Prime Minister did realize some modest achievements in terms of the transformation of the socio-economic infrastructure, for the most part, he was unable to deliver the widespread sweeping revolutionary changes he had earlier advocated. While it is possible that his intentions may well have been noble and genuinely worked towards the transformation of the condition of the working class, economic constraints and a lack of working capital seriously curtailed his ability to initiate programs of reform and deliver on his promises. Certainly, natural disasters which impacted on and somewhat altered Bishop's ability to transform the nation's economy, coupled with the inheritance of an unsound economy from Gairy, were circumstances beyond his control and, one might well argue, that Bishop should not be blamed for this. While there is, however, some validity to this assertion, the fact is that the condition of working class Grenadians remained basically the same under Bishop as it was under

Gairy. Nothing had really changed despite Bishop's many promises. Bishop was clearly either unable or unwilling to transform the socio-economic sector of the country. Working class Grenadians began seriously to question his ability and willingness as Prime Minister and principal leader of the nation to implement change. Thus, for the first time since the start of the revolution, Bishop's integrity, and commitment to implement national societal reform, began to be scrutinized by working class elements of the society that had earlier firmly supported him in his bid for power. Grenadians were no longer certain about the man or the revolution they had helped to create. The perception they had of their chosen leader was now beginning to waiver.

The increasing negative perception Grenadians began developing of Bishop was apparently reinforced by certain actions of the latter which followed. Before his ascent to power, Bishop promised Grenadians that there would be national elections in the country. After he assumed power, however, no national elections were held. In fact, in the four and one half years that the N.J.M.'s leadership controlled the political reins of the country, very little discussion and virtually no concrete attempt was ever made to restore a system of elections on the island. While there was some indication that Bishop might have eventually embarked upon a system of "open and free" elections, the fact is that he had not kept his promise to the Grenadian citizenry to transform the political infrastructure of the island, despite what Grenadians considered to be ample time for him to have done so.

Bishop clearly reneged on his promise. Once again he failed to deliver on the promises he made to the Grenadian masses. His failure to transform the political sector and hold "open and free elections" was, as Grenadians saw it, yet another example of his inability, unwillingness, and/or lack of commitment to accomplish the goals he had set himself and the promises he had made to his people. Suffice to say that these failures only helped to reinforce in the minds of Grenadians the negative image they were now beginning to develop of him.

The Grenadians' unfavorable perception of the N.J.M.'s leadership quickly became firmly entrenched through certain actions which followed. Subsequent to attaining political power, Bishop promised to restore justice and democracy to the island. He advocated freedom of the press, freedom of religion, and non-infringement of government on the political rights of the local citizenry.

While these promises were noble gestures on his part it is, however, quite clear by now that he did not abide by them. Once in power, his actions were very much to the contrary. He forcefully closed down the press, infringed on the political rights of Grenadians, antagonized local churches and the clergy, and rounded up and jailed thousands of people.[5] These were not the actions one would expect from the leader of a country who had promised justice and democracy. These actions were merely denying the people of Grenada basic human rights that are characteristic of any true democracy. Despite his promised ideals Bishop had in effect created, whether manifestly or latently, a totalitarian state in which he and the other key members of the N.J.M.'s leadership were in total control. The N.J.M. had ruled with an oppressive hand, and oppression was clearly the order of the day. This fact was evident in his use of torture, physical force, and sometimes even death to silence those who opposed him and his totalitarian regime or the things they believed in.[5] Given the condition of the Grenadian working class, generating "Bucks" would have aided the process of alleviating their socio-economic condition. The "Bible" too, could have been used as a symbol of forgiveness for those who opposed him. It may well have been the Christian thing to do, given that he advocated justice and freedom of religion, and wanted to bring the Grenadian working class under the control of one.

Grenadians' suspicion and distrust of the N.J.M.'s political leadership, coupled with their increasing lack of identification with it, was made most profound by the military course of action Bishop and Deputy Prime Minister Bernard Coard pursued. Once in power, Bishop and Coard embarked upon a huge military build-up. They also quickly signed secret military agreements with communist-bloc countries, and were building a military airport under the disguise of a commerical one.[6] The emergent actions of the N.J.M.'s leadership, therefore, were carefully designed to transform the socio-economic and political infrastructure of the island: these leaders were systematically changing the country from an alleged democracy under Gairy to a military and totalitarian state.

These actions point to a number of things. First, a military buildup meant that socialism was beginning to make serious inroads into the country. Second, an ever increasing foreign presence on the island[7] would culminate in decreasing autonomy and thus reduce Grenadian influence in and control of domestic affairs. In other words, an increasing foreign presence on the island would proportionately increase its dominance[7] and control of the Grenadian masses.

Third it alludes to Bishop's secrecy and withholding of information from the Grenadian public. The fact that Bishop did not inform his citizenry of military agreements and the arms build-up course of action he had embarked upon, leads one to speculate that such news would not have been welcomed by the Grenadian public and was perhaps, the fundamental reason why they were not informed. Bishop and Coard might have anticipated public resentment and reprisal and were thus fearful of it, particularly the degree to which it could have undermined their popularity.

A fourth implication of Bishop's actions was that he was transforming a democratic plantation-oriented society into a socialist one through the revolutionary process: he was quickly and quite radically changing the social, economic, and political structure of the island from one extreme to the other, was instituting a new way of life that Grenadians were not used to, and, chances are, would not accept. Bishop wanted to destroy the plantation system and replace it with a new social order. He realized that, historically. the plantation system had denied Grenadians a "real stake in their country."[6] It had created "A chronic dependency syndrome" that was "characteristic of the whole population."[8] And, "people are not sufficiently motivated to make sacrifices and to expend efforts."[8] Thus, only by destroying the system can the legacies of plantation society be overcome.[8] As he envisioned it, destroying the system would involve "revolutionary change in the institutional structure",[8] and this was precisely the course of action he embarked upon in an attempt to be consistent with his ideological outlook.

While Bishop's concerns may have been genuine, the course of action he pursued negatively impacted on the Grenadian citizenry. Although plantation society was a closed and rigid system, and was repressive,[9] yet it was the form of society Grenadians knew best, and they were not prepared to tolerate any other. Despite its inhibitions, plantation society was at least democratic and it was a form of life Grenadians had grown accustomed to over the years. With Bishop in power, democracy quickly began becoming something of the past. This meant that the lives of Grenadians were abruptly disrupted. The uprooting of the old system and the institution of a new one through the process of radical change signalled a sudden and unwelcomed transformation in their lives. Thus, it was precisely this attempt to politically transform the society, and the way Bishop went about doing so, that culminated in a certain alienation of the masses from him and the revolution and had Grenadians believing that they had jumped from the " frying pan" under Gairy, "into the fire" under Bishop. The once popular leader,

Bishop, had betrayed them. Both leader and revolution, therefore, were to be opposed.

Indeed, the March 13 revolution was changing the social, political and economic structure of Grenada. The input of socialism meant that the democratic constitution of the island was suspended.[2] To the government, as it had overtly boasted, "March 13 was the biggest election Grenada ever had."[2] While many Grenadians initially supported the N.J.M. in its removal of Gairy, they soon realized that the latter could not solve the socio-economic and political problems of the island. This realization was aggravated by Bishop's repressive hand, something that was most unwelcomed by the masses. In alluding to this in an interview with one of the authors, a Grenadian living in New York, prior to the U.S. invasion of the island, lamented, "Ruling the country with the gun is against what most of us want. If this continues, there would continue to be several attempts to counter-revolution. . . Democracy under Gairy might not have worked but it was much better than what we have today. How many of us can stand up today in the market square and tell Bishop he is no good?"[2] Another commented, "I have just returned from Grenada. . . there is a certain amount of fear in Grenada. People are afraid to talk about the government for fear that they might be arrested by the People's Revolutionary Army. In order to speak to relatives I had to visit their homes at night. Grenadians are not used to this. I wish the government would realize this."[2] These interviews are quite revealing. Other than expressing dissatifaction with the existing state of affairs in Grenada at the time, they lend support to the fact that Bishop was tearing down firmly established institutional structures and replacing them with radically new ones. Socialism was an alien ideology; it was imported and, as Grenadians saw it, certainly not conducive to that society. Resentment and overt antagonism towards it, therefore, was more the natural order of things. In addition, Grenadians tended to doubt Bishop's verbal commitment to moderate means, and this doubt culminated in a certain amount of alienation and detachment from both the N.J.M.'s leadership and the revolution on the whole.

## Time Frame Three: October 13, 1983 to October 25, 1983 and Beyond

During this third period, an internal power struggle between Maurice Bishop and Bernard Coard was exacerbated. It culminated in the bloody assassination of the former, and paved the way for both the military coup that followed and the subsequent establishment of a ruling military junta.

A power struggle within the ranks of the N.J.M. must be assessed for its wider implications. There are a number of things that can be addressed here. In the first place, an internal power struggle reflected a lack of consensus on the part of the leadership. The inability of the leaders to work together and arrive at some degree of consensus, indicates that they were unable to agree on political philosophy and/or ideology and were thus unclear about the aims, ideals, and purposes of the revolution, as well as the course it should pursue. Second, given the lack of organizational clarity and purpose on the part of the leadership, it was unable to fully achieve its goals. Organizational clarity and purpose is a necessary prerequisite for goal attainment and it can sometimes aid or deter organizational effectiveness.

The third point is that the waging of an internal power struggle caused the revolution to suffer. Conflict, competition, and overt antagonism between Maurice Bishop and Bernard Coard emanated because each of these men wanted to satisfy and perpetuate his own selfish and reactionary interests. So much time was spent by each man in an attempt to outdo the other that each had no time left, if even he wanted, to coordinate organizational activities. Because of the pursuit of personal gain, the concerns of the revolution were left both unaddressed and unattended; therefore, it suffered in the sense that it was unable to forge ahead.

Fourth, the neglect of revolutionary concerns on the part of leadership was directly responsible for putting Grenada in a very vulnerable position. An internal power struggle meant that little or no time was spent defending the revolution from foreign invasion which was always a constant threat.

The fifth point, which necessarily follows from the fourth, is that an internal power struggle left the doors wide open for the U.S. invasion of the island. The power struggle between Bishop and Coard subsequently climaxed with a bloody military coup which put the country in a state of disorganization and chaos. In fact, it was precisely this existing state of affairs that prompted the U.S. to take swift military action. The coup had presented President Reagan with that long awaited moment; it served as the single most important factor that paved the way for the U.S. invasion of the island. The U.S. had, after all, quickly capitalized on the existing political situation in Grenada and, beyond a doubt, this had tipped the scale towards the side of Washington. In an article in The New York Times titled "Castro Says the Coup in Grenada 'Opened Doors' to

U.S. Invasion", it was reported, "President Fidel Castro, denouncing the United States invasion of Grenada, said today that it came only after the men who had overthrown and killed Prime Minister Maurice Bishop 'sank the revolution and opened the doors to imperialist aggression'."[10] The report continued to note that Castro "took pains to explain that the revolution in Grenada had ended before United States troops landed at the airport that Cubans were helping to build at Point Salines."[10] In his words, "the revolution could not have survived the internal struggle led by Deputy Prime Minister Bernard Coard and that the symbol of progress and independence that Grenada had become had been destroyed already."[10]

Castro's analysis is correct. Other than alluding to the lack of consensus and cohesion on the part of the N.J.M.'s leadership and its inability to work together for the success of the revolution, his analysis clearly establishes that the Grenada revolution was destroyed from within. Bernard Coard, one of the key leaders of the N.J.M. and also Deputy Prime Minister, had betrayed the revolution. Although he was opposed to the United States his action served as a latent function in that, while not intended, his betrayal of Maurice Bishop inadvertently and unintentionally assisted the U.S. in the invasion of the island.

The fact that Bernard Coard was able to betray Maurice Bishop and, thus, destroy the revolution, points to some serious shortcomings on the part of Bishop. On October 19, 1983, the day of the assassination of Bishop, it was Bernard Coard who had the support of the military and not Maurice Bishop. Ever since his ascent to the political position as Deputy Prime Minister, Coard had maintained close ties with the military, especially with its top-ranking officers. In fact, most of the top-ranking officers of the military were ardent supporters and followers of Coard and his ideological outlook, and belonged to his political faction of the N.J.M. This meant that Coard could have manipulated the military in any which way he wanted, and actually did so. In addition, the military's loyalty was to Coard. Meanwhile Bishop, very much unlike Coard, ignored the military and neglected to build up a support structure within its ranks. Despite his alleged initial concern for the militia, as well as his ranting advocacy of such, indications are that he did not work closely with the military and thus failed to establish close ties with it during his entire term in political office. This meant a certain separation and distance between him and the military which was crucial in terms of contributing to the latter's sense of loyalty to Coard and not to Bishop in the end.

Bishop's inability to maintain close ties with the military and thus command its loyalty demonstrates a serious miscalculation and/or oversight on his part. It would seem that the military was perhaps unimportant to him, and his very behavior seemed to have confirmed this despite what he said in the initial stages of the revolution. Bishop had apparently overlooked the warnings of Lenin that, in any revolution, the military is both vital and necessary for the protection and perpetuation of the revolution. In countries where the legitimacy of the incumbent political government is threatened either by popular uprising or by dissident political factions, it is the military that is generally sent out to suppress the people on behalf of the government. Therefore, it is mandatory that political incumbents in revolutionary and totalitarian states maintain close ties with the military in an attempt to procure its allegiance, support, and sense of loyalty when it is needed. Bishop had underestimated or overlooked the crucial function the military was capable of playing in the defense of the revolution and, in a sense, had alienated himself from it. This was perhaps the fundamental reason why he was unable to procure its tacit support at a time when it was most needed to put down the armed uprising by Bernard Coard's faction of the N.J.M., an uprising that culminated in the bloody overthrow of Bishop himself. Meanwhile Bernard Coard who, very much unlike Bishop, neither overlooked nor underestimated the importance of the military in the revolutionary process and who all along maintained close ties with it, was able to use it to his fullest advantage.

Coard's ability to command the military's support towards the end of the revolution, also exposes Bishop's failure to monitor and scrutinize Coard's actions. Not only had Coard maintained close ties with the military but also, over the years, developed a powerful support base within its ranks. Coard was able to accomplish this base only because Bishop allowed him both excessive autonomy and power with the military and left it unchecked. Also, Bishop was either unaware of or underestimated the intensity of support the military had for Coard and the degree of allegiance and loyalty it owed to the Deputy Prime Minister.

The implications of Bishop's shortcomings exposes the inherent weakness of his leadership capabilities. He either considered the connection between Coard and the military as being unimportant and thus dismissed it too perfunctorily or as something that was not significant enough to pose a serious threat to his regime. This oversight, of course, altered his ability to explore further Coard's relationship with the military, and what it might mean in terms of undermining his privileged position, while at the same time enhancing Coard's. Without the military, Coard was powerless. With the military Coard was powerful, and he proved that on October 19, the day the military stood on his side and bloodily did away with Maurice Bishop and his incumbent political faction of the N.J.M.

Increasing power with the military on the part of Coard that was left unchecked or ruled out as being insignificant by the Prime Minister, had inadvertently worked to his disadvantage: it culminated in the demise and downfall of the later. Thus, in a very real sense Bishop, because of his actions, had contributed to his own failure.

An examination and analysis of Bishop's actions clearly indicates that he was not the charismatic and cunning leader Grenadians initially thought he was. As Prime Minister, Bishop was unable to fulfill the aspirations, satisfy the demands, and alleviate the condition of the working class. As the principal leader of the N.J.M., he was unable to hold the party together. He also neglected the essential leadership function of monitoring the actions of all party members, particularly those of Bernard Coard. What we see then is that "externally", that is in the eyes of Grenadians, Bishop had failed as a leader. "Internally", that is as principal leader of the N.J.M., he also failed because he was unable to hold the N.J.M. together. He either lacked the leadership skills, was unware of them, and/or ignored the role he should play within the status he occupied. Thus, it would seem that his lack of leadership qualities had reversed his initial charismatic appeal and had obviously contributed to both his own downfall and the revolution's failure.

The final point that can be made with respect to our examination and analysis of the actions of the leadership is that not having a second line of leadership to carry on the struggle marked the demise of the N.J.M. and the revolution. Subsequent to the U.S. invasion of the island and the arrest and imprisonment of the key leaders, there was not a designated second line of leadership to pursue the revolution and put up an armed struggle against the invading forces. Both Bishop and Coard, while in power, had neglected to appoint a second line of leadership in an attempt to co-ordinate party activities and give directions in the absence or untimely death of top party officials. When the U.S. forces invaded and either killed or captured top party leaders, the revolution readily folded. Let us indicate that one of the most widely known and commonly adopted counter-revolutionary political strategies is either the killing, arrest, and/or imprisonment of the popular and sometimes charismatic leadership of such a revolution, because it is such leadership that continuously co-ordinates activities, maintains cohesiveness and infuses the revolution with organizational direction and commitment to purpose.[1] Depriving the movement of its leadership thus weakens its organizational effectiveness. Consequently, if there is no designation of a second line of leadership to continue the struggle, subsequent to the killing and/or arrest and imprisonment of its principal leaders, the revolution cannot remain cohesive and viable for long and tends to fall apart in the face of armed insurgence.[1] Suffice to say that this calamity is precisely what happened in the Grenadian situation.

# CHAPTER SIX

# CONCLUSION

Our primary concern in this book, as we noted in the Introduction, has been to ascertain why the Grenada revolution failed. Throughout the study, this was the fundamental issue we addressed. Our examination and analysis of this revolution, therefore, tended to depict and explore questions that revolved around key issues of the revolution that, in our opinion, were in some way related to its demise. Thus, in this concluding chapter, we will bring together the multiplicity of reasons we have outlined that coalesced to culminate in the failure of the Grenada revolution, and speak to their wider sociological implications.

Before we summarize the reasons why the Grenada revolution failed, it will be necessary to outline some of the promises that the N.J.M. made to Grenadians. In its manifesto, the N.J.M. promised the following: (1) To carry out the wishes of the people, (2) To improve the quality of life for all Grenadians, (3) And, to create a national political climate where Grenadians could live free of fear, hunger, misery and exploitation.

We have argued throughout this book that the revolution failed because it was unable to achieve the goals and objectives that were stated in the N.J.M.'s manifesto. Let us, therefore, examine what was done to achieve these goals and objectives.

**Broken Promises**

Bishop's inability to keep his promise was one of the main reasons why the Grenada revolution failed. Subsequent to obtaining power, Bishop promised free and open elections and a reverting back to a system of true democracy. In his radio address to the people of Grenada on March 13, 1979, he declared that a government would be formed from all the elements that were opposed to Gairy: that elections would be held in the early future, and that all political parties would be free to hold meetings.

Why weren't elections held? Bishop was more concerned with socialist rule rather than with a system of democracy and elections. Although he told Grenadians that he was committed to delivering them from the tyranny of Gairy, his actions, if anything, were more in line with a political doctrine that deviated from a truly free society. His promises on March 13, 1979, were merely political propaganda used to capitalize on the existing situation at the time. His actions, however, were something else. They were designed to perpetuate the things he and the N.J.M. believed in rather than fulfill the political wishes of the people who had helped him remove Eric Gairy from political office. While it is true that Grenadians wanted to change the then present government, this in no way is to suggest that they were opting for a political system oriented towards socialism. The data that we collected clearly indicates that the major concern of Grenadians was to remove Gairy from political office but continue in the democratic tradition. Only a handful of those we interviewed indicated they would have preferred a socialist form of government. The mass support the N.J.M. received between 1974 and 1979 was a result of frustration with Gairy. Grenadians were also responding to the images of Gairy that were presented by the N.J.M. The former truly believed that once Gairy was removed, the N.J.M. would continue with a democratic system as it had promised, but as we know, it did not.

**Was the Education System Improved?**

Despite the P.R.G.'s rhetoric and claims of success, it is clear that the lack of organization, sacrifice and curriculm development led to a downward trend in education. It was not uncommon to hear students of the leading high schools in Grenada say that "the white man's education is intended to enslave us... true liberation can only come from the barrel of a gun.", This attitude, coupled with the mass resignation of many high school principals, let to a marked decline in the number of students who passed the General Certificate of Education (G.C.E.) and the local School Leaving Examination. The G.C.E. is awarded to students who have completed Form Five and who are able to pass an external examination. The School Leaving, on the other hand, is given to students who have completed Standard Seven and who are able to pass the local examination given by the Ministry of Education. In 1981, roughly two years after the Grenada revolution, 2318 students passed the School Leaving Examination. The School Leaving Examination is equivalent to tenth grade in America. In 1983, only 1584 students passed this examination. It should be pointed out that the number of students in the primary schools who took the School Leaving Examination had increased.

A look at the results of the G.C.E. Ordinary level (O) and the Advanced level (A) tells a similar story. In 1981 five students passed the G.C.E. A level with three or more subjects. In 1983, the number of students who received four or more G.C.E. O level passes was 110. In 1983, the number of the G.C.E. candidates who received four or more O level passes had dropped to 93. In 1981, the number of passes had dropped to 3. In 1981, 23 candidates successfully completed the G.C.E. A level with one pass. In 1983, fifteen students received at least one pass. An examination of the Ministry of Education statistical report indicates that the number of students who attempted the G.C.E., O level and A level between 1980 and 1983, had increased.

Many Grenadians, especially those who had access to this statistical information, realized that the goals and objectives of the revolution were not being achieved. Several questioned the aims and objectives of the P.R.G. Needless to say, those who dared question Bishop's government were imprisoned, threatened, or had their personal property seized.

**Economic Crisis**

The revolution was also plagued by a severe economic crisis. Immediately following the rise of Bishop to political power, he promised Grenadians that the revolution would bring food, and alleviate the oppressed condition of the working class. But the revolution did not bring food, neither did it transform the socio-economic infrastructure of the island.[2] The revolution merely meant the displacing of an old political regime and the institution of a new one. The need for "bread" and social amenities was as widespread under Bishop as it was under Gairy. Grenadians continued to go hungry. Foodstuffs remained in short supply and fundamental but yet vital and necessary social services were lacking, inadequate or unavailable. Conditions of deprivation continued to be the order of the day, and the masses were merely scrambling for scarce resources.

Added to this state is that Grenada was hit by economic hardtimes. The island experienced a major recession under Bishop; it was faced with a shrinking economy. Grenada was importing most of its food and manufactured goods and producing virtually nothing. Its national earnings fell and its national deficit increased significantly. Grenada was also hit with a number of hurricanes, rainstorms, and floods which destroyed the economic mainstays of the island.[3] These natural disasters only served to retard further development of the national economy.

This meant that while Bishop's concern for national socio-economic growth might have been genuine, he simply did not have the resources to bring it about. His hands were tied, and the promises he made to the Grenadian people could not be fulfilled. Bishop was certainly in a precarious position. He had promised something but could not deliver. Not having the financial resources to institute systems of socio-economic reform, his promises became mere rhetoric and false hopes. He quickly realized that internal economic feasibility is the crucial and necessary element for national reform. Given the lack of economic resources, he turned to the communist-bloc countries for economic aid. The monies Bishop received were merely "a drop in the bucket" and they were allocated primarily for military purposes. Bishop's inability to reform the economy of the island and alleviate the conditions of the working class, even with the assistance of foreign aid, prompted a certain negative assessment on the part of Grenadians towards him and his regime, and ultimately served to both condition their perception of this once popular revolution and the degree to which they identified with it in the end.

**Was Freedom Achieved?**

Bishop's commitment was not necessarily one that was geared toward promoting freedom and democracy as he claimed but, instead, his real intent was to build up the military and create a political system where the state would assume total control of the society: he would have a militia ready to perpetuate and defend state interests from both internal and external aggression and this is why he spent so much time and effort doing so. While talking about a truly free and democratic society might have been noble ideals, he was actually not committed to it. He was using it as a political ploy to secure his own position with the Grenadian masses and conceal his revolutionary motives.

The oppressive measures of the P.R.G. did little to enhance this group's public image. In fact, it gave Grenadians an opportunity to compare and contrast Bishop's leadership with that of Gairy. It came to be generally accepted that Gairy's tyrannical rule was mild compared to that of the P.R.G.'s Mrs. U.V. told the authors that, "Gairy's Mongoose Gang couldn't carry water for Bishop's Secret Police... these guys (meaning the Secret Police) are trained and vicious criminals."[4] The oppressive measures, threats, personal injury and victimization served as deterrents in the early stages of the revolution. The effects of these measures were reduced as Grenadians realized that the revolution was "heading in the wrong direction". The hostile measures of the P.R.G., instead of generating fear as it once did, now created a feeling of hostility against the revolution. These concerns, as they saw it, represented a society that was closed and overtly repressive. Meanwhile, despite its alleged inhibitions, plantation society was very much an open system that advocated democratic ideals, and one that Grenadians had grown accustomed to over the years. They were, therefore, not prepared to abdicate it for some form of political rule that they were both unsure about and resented. Bishop's political ideals were not democratic in outlook, neither did they represent freedom of thought and expression - ideals that have conditioned the lives of Grenadians and ones they have held on dearly to. As Grenadians saw it, the political path that Bishop had chosen was very much opposed and in contrast to the ideals of democracy. It advocated a new way of life that was oriented toward tearing down established institutional structures and replacing them with totally new and radically different ones.

**The Use of Force**

One way to insure the continued success of such an alien ideology was through force. The P.R.G. used every means at its disposal to silence so-called destabilizers. A member of the Central Committee told the authors that they had to do something drastic to demonstrate to Grenadians and the world that the revolution meant business. Their first major decision, according to this informant, was to silence Bishop. He said, "the brother (meaning Bishop) thought his popularity placed him above the revolution... Our asking him to share power with Coard was to demonstrate to him and to the world that no one is above the heavy hand of the revolution. Our revolution will continue regardless of personal and ideological differences."[4]

By using these punitive measures, the revolution lost most of its popular support. To regain that support, Bishop decided to make certain overtures to the landed gentry, the merchants, the elite, and the peasant proprietors. His last but unsuccessful visit to the U.S. to engage in open dialogue with President Reagan was an attempt to regain the confidence of the elite class and to legitimize his government. Bishop realized that Grenada was a closed society and, therefore, Grenadians looked to certain members in their communities for leadership and advice. If the revolution was to succeed, it could not continue to alienate these leaders. An informant and a high ranking former member of the N.J.M. told the authors on their recent visit to Grenada that "the P.R.G. was unable to deal with theory and practice... they were unable to develop a workable synthesis."₅

The data which the authors collected indicates that Bishop's and the P.R.G.'s inability to apply successfully the Marxist-Leninist doctrine to Grenada and their unawareness of and/or unwillingness to deal with theory and practice were responsible for the demise and eventual failure of the revolution. Grenadians in Grenada who dared criticize the P.R.G. were placed "under heavy manners". Grenadians abroad who criticized the revolution were threatened or had their relatives who lived in Grenada victimized. During this reign of terror, comments like these were quite popular: "Boy ah better keep me mouth shut.. you know ah have me children and relative still in the man country"; "wah we go do girl, the people have the guns and Mr. Castro stand behind them"; "Ah use to tell you all dat... those boys (meaning the P.R.G.) are no damn good". By the latter half of 1982 and all of 1983, Grenadians everywhere were beginning to assert themselves and to present a combative attitude toward the revolution. The people's feelings of helplessness and despair were replaced by anger and a determination to restore democracy to Grenada. In Brooklyn, the "march for freedom" was led by the Grenada Movement for Freedom and Democracy (G.M.F.D.). The leader of the G.M.F.D. and other members of the organization openly demonstrated against the atrocities of the P.R.G. This organization was prepared to "fight fire with fire". It even hinted some type of military intervention against the P.R.G. Like the N.J.M. in the mid-70's, the G.M.F.D. was respected and feared.

### Why Impression Management Failed

Probably the most successful instrument used by the P.R.G. was its ability to manage impressions. Between 1979 and 1982, the P.R.G., like Gairy between 1951 and 1974, controlled center stage. It used its propaganda machinery to create images that other Caribbean leaders envied. Any semblance of failure was blamed on the evils of capitalism. The P.R.G. refused to take any of the blame for a failing economy, poor roads, housing, medical facilities, and the lowering of the educational standards. Whenever they appeared publicly, the members of the P.R.G. did everything in their power to protect the private image of the revolution. A well organized, well financed, well planned, and well administered propaganda machinery was developed to present the public image of the revolution. Its aims were (1) to silence any form of opposition, public or private. The P.R.G. accomplished these aims by closing the local newspapers, by actively seeking favorable coverage in the foreign press, and by infiltrating fraternal and social organizations at home and abroad. For example, the membership of the two oldest Grenadian organizations in Brooklyn increased between 1980 and 1982. The new members of these organizations were younger and somewhat better educated. The P.R.G. sought and successfully replaced officers in these organizations who did not support its program. (2) To instill fear and helplessness in the minds of all Grenadians. The purpose here was to posit the revolution as something powerful and strong and therefore could not be turned back. From 1979 to about 1982, Grenadians were afraid to speak or write about the revolution.

But before long, the P.R.G. was unable to adequately manage the private image of the revolution. Especially after 1981, it was unable to manage the impressions that pointed to the failures of the revolution.

## The Lack of Ideological Clarity

From very early on the revolution lacked a central focus. Two separate approaches emerged. The Bishop faction advocated popular support and saw their leader's charisma as being sufficient to sustain the revolution. With this in mind, it developed and propogated two images of the revolution, the private and the public. The private image was well guarded. Political, ideological and personal differences were kept away from the public.

The P.R.G. was, by the middle of 1982, experiencing internal struggles over ideological clarity, political direction, international criticism, economic isolation, and local and regional criticism. How did the P.R.G. deal with these problems? The data indicates that there were two separate and distinct approaches. Bishop advocated a return to the "Westminister Model" which he vehemently opposed in 1979. The supporters of Bernard Coard saw this move toward parliamentary democracy as a return to Gairyism in Grenada, and thus opposed it. In its place, they advocated a Marxist-Leninist approach. The rational here was that the revolution was strong enough to withstand economic pressures and criticism from capitalist countries. In the September 25, 1983, meeting of the Central Committee it was advocated that the party adopt a Leninist level of organization and discipline, develop ideological clarity, and exercise Leninist supervision. By this time Bishop had no real control over the members of the Central Committee, and was simply following their dictates. The members of the Central Committee decided that the revolution would succeed regardless of ideological differences, but it did not.

## P.R.G. Leadership Attacked

By the middle of 1982, Bishop's government was criticized in Grenada and abroad. In Grenada his leadership was under attack by Bernard Coard's supporters on the Central Committee. The Prime Minister's visit to the United States, his appointment of a commission to draw up a constitution in preparation for elections, and his concessions to the bourgeoisie class were severely criticised by certain members of the Central Committee who wanted Grenada to follow a Marxist-Leninist path. The P.R.G. was also attacked by foreign governments. America openly accused the Bishop regime of transporting terrorism to the Caribbean and condemned Grenada's friendship with Cuba. President Reagan in one of his national television broadcasts, said the new international airport being built at Point Salines would be used by Cuba and her allies to transport military hardware and terrorism to the Caribbean and to other Third World countries. Several Caribbean leaders, by this time, were openly opposed to the P.R.G. Eugenia Charles of Dominica, Edward Seaga of Jamaica, Tom Adams of Barbados, and George Chambers of Trinidad, to name a few, saw the massive buildup of military hardware in Grenada as a destabilizing force in the Caribbean. Several Caribbean leaders saw the Grenada experiment as a threat to both their political careers and the stability of their countries. A Caribbean Prime Minister recently told the authors that "with Grenada around, none of us felt safe... not only did we have to worry about building schools for our children, or roads for our farmers, but we also have to concentrate on building and strengthening our military ... the Grenada experiment had become a nightmare for all of us."[6]

## Personality Politics

An article in the Grenadian Voice, adequately summarized one of our findings when it said that "Bishop, because of his personality was, in the eyes of the people, the revolution... it would seem in the end that despite all the rhetoric and re-education the people resorted to personality politics in supporting Bishop and not the revolution."[7] The members of the Central Committee spent too much of their time comparing their leader, Maurice Bishop, with Eric Gairy. In a recent interview with a former supporter of the P.R.G., she told us that, "one of the serious mistakes of the P.R.G. was their continual criticism of Gairy... The more Bishop compared his leadership abilities with Gairy, the more the Grenadians realized that Gairy was not at all that bad." Gairy was seen as a leader who could have been trusted and respected. Bishop, on the other hand, was now viewed as one who couldn't be trusted. Thus the death blow to the revolution was struck when Grenadians parted company with Bishop, the man. Bishop had inadvertently helped to undermine his own position by comparing himself with Gairy.

## The Main Blow to the Revolution

By 1983 it had become clear that there were open hostilities and confrontations between the Coards and the Bishops. Maurice Bishop, the Prime Minister, realized that his deputy, Bernard Coard, wanted to share power. It is also common knowledge that Angela and Phyllis despised each other. These confrontations between Maurice and Bernard on the one hand, and their wives Angela and Phyllis on the other, led to a clear division among the members of the Central Committee. The supporters of Coard opted for a rapid reorganization of the socio-economic and political infrastructure of the island while the supporters of Bishop wanted slow and gradual change. It was these differences in ideologies, political and social directions that, more than anything else, were responsible for the arrest and subsequent killing of Bishop, and the demise of the revolution on the whole.

## Armed Might of the United States

The failure of the Grenada revolution must also be attributed to the armed might of the United States. By armed might we mean sheer military strength. The United States is a formidable military power. Many would argue that the United States is perhaps the most powerful military nation in the world. What does military power have to do with the crushing of a revolution? Military power is one of the most essential characteristics needed to crush a revolution. Superior military hardware, skilled military manpower, and military strategy are essential assets to the process of the defeat of revolutionary forces, particularly in situations where the opposition lacks those vital and necessary armaments to put up an armed struggle in an attempt to thwart outside military aggression and thus protect the revolution. Grenada was certainly not in a position to counter the military might of the United States. It would be merely foolish to argue that Grenada's military capabilities can be matched with that of the United States. Grenada is a tiny island with little national defense capabilities. Even with Cuban and Soviet aid, the island is by no means militarily equivalent to the United States. Russian and Cuban aid, as well as their military presence on the island, would have made it more difficult for the United States to invade but certainly not impossible. The United States was apparently confident that, given its military superiority, it could crush the revolution and this was another reason that prompted it to take the type of action it did. Given that its timing of the invasion could not have been better, it was absolutely confident that its military strength as a world power would aid rather than alter the process of a successful invasion. In situations where there is a test of strength between two contending military factions, the one that possesses superior military capabilities will almost invariably and inevitably crush the opposing faction. History has attested to this all too readily. In situations where world powers have engaged in warfare, the possession of superior military hardware and skilled military manpower is essential to the defeat of the opposition. Military superiority has, more often than not, been an essential variable in determining the outcome of warfare, and in the Grenada revolution it was no different in that this quality possessed by the United States was essential to the defeat of that revolution and the tipping of the scale to the side of Washington.

**Barring of U.S. News Reporters**

The fact that American news reporters were barred from Grenada during the invasion and thus unable to report on it, also impacted on the revolution's outcome. Prior to the military coup on the island, American reporters were expelled from Grenada by Prime Minister Bishop. Also, American troops, acting on orders from the U.S. military, forcefully prevented reporters from entering the country during the invasion. This meant that despite freedom of the press and the importance of the story, the American news media was barred from the scene of military action and was thus unable to report on the invasion. Barring the news media was apparently designed either to impose a news blackout on the Grenada situation, or at least screen and filter the information that was reported on it.

What did the barring of U.S. reporters from the island during the invasion have to do with the revolution's failure? We contend that the barring of news reporters from and the imposition of a news blackout on the island was crucial to American military success. This action on the part of the United States meant that it could have engaged in strategic military action on the island without fear of such news reaching the outside world, particularly the communist and socialist world, thus deterring the possibility of outside military aid being rushed to Grenada in an attempt to enhance its chances for a successful military defense.

## Arrest and Imprisonment of Leaders

The final reason that contributed to the revolution's failure is the arrest and imprisonment of its leaders. The arrest and subsequent imprisonment of the leaders, particularly Bernard Coard and Hudson Austin, in the later stages of the American invasion, meant that the revolution did not have an organized "second line" of leadership to carry on the struggle. Historically, one of the most widely known and commonly adopted counter-revolutionary strategies is the arrest and imprisonment of the popular and sometimes charismatic leadership of a revolution because it is such leadership that continuously co-ordinates activities, maintains cohesiveness and infuses the revolution with direction and commitment to purpose. Depriving the revolution of its leadership weakens it organizational effectiveness. Thus, if there is no designation of a "second line" of leadership to continue the struggle subsequent to the arrest and imprisonment of its principal leaders, the revolution cannot remain cohesive and viable for long and tends to fall apart in the face of armed military might. Leadership's inability to designate a "second line" of leadership, shows that it either overlooked or ignored the consequences of this, particularly in situations where the revolution would have to militarily defend itself against both external and internal forces. Thus, not designating a second line of leadership, despite its commitment to protect the revolution, indicates that leadership had not firmly established the revolution as a functional and viable organization capable of protecting itself from armed insurgence, and so inadvertently made it more vulnerable to being crushed as it eventually was by invading U.S. forces.

## Some Parting Thoughts

Even though this study was exploratory in nature it, nevertheless, demonstrated that the Marxist form of government is not the answer to Third World countries such as those of the Caribbean. Grenadians and other Caribbean peoples are more concerned with their day to day survival than with ideological and political doctrines. Given this it would seem that for any form of government in this region to succeed, it must offer the people a better way of life by assisting them in their everyday concerns rather than expending its efforts on the choice of political models and ideology. As we have seen, ideological rhetoric on the part of the P.R.G., did not solve the socio-economic and political problems of Grenadians. Instead, all it did was offer a sense of hope and security which, as we know, the revolution was unable to fulfill. In short, the food, housing, and better social services that the N.J.M. promised during its campaign against Gairy, were not achieved. Thus, the Grenada revolution failed because of its inability to get at the ways that Grenadians define their reality. This simply suggests that politicians and social thinkers will not get at real meanings if they assume what the realities of the people are and act only on that assumption. Members of the P.R.G. were puzzled when they found out that their hopes, dreams and aspirations for Grenada were quite different than those of the masses, the people that they claimed to represent.

What we have done in this study is attempt to outline the reasons why the Grenada revolution failed. While we have attempted to indicate the reasons for the failure of this once popular revolution, this study in no way exhausts other possible explanations. Further analysis of additional variables and other explanatory factors are needed to broaden our knowledge and understanding of this crucial process. Given the exploratory nature of this study, it underscores the need for some adequate theoretical framework to explain why already instituted, popular revolutions in Third World countries do oftentimes reach the point of unpopularity and thus subject themselves to failure. The study also highlights the need for research that would address itself to the concerns of what revolutionary leaders in Third World countries can do to secure the stability of revolutions, thus allowing them to cohere and succeed.

Today, discussion about the Grenada revolution continues. One thing is clear and that is that this revolution was unable to build the new society which it talked about: it was unable to create a workable synthesis acceptable to all Grenadians. The revolution that successfully ousted the Gairy regime from political power in 1979 had, therefore, failed miserably some four and one half years later.

# REFERENCES AND NOTES

## Introduction

1. **Caribbean Review,** Vol. XII, No. 4, Fall 1983, pp. 14-15.

2. Tony Bilton, et.al., **Introductory Sociology** London: The Mac Millian Press Ltd. 1981, p. 639.

3. D. Sinclair Dabreo, **The Grenada Revolution** (St. Lucia: M.A.P.S., Publication, 1979), p. 61.

4. Niccolo Machiavelli, **The Prince** (New York: The New American Library, 1952), p.50.

5. Interview with Mr. B.B., August, 1979.

6. Interview with Mr. H.S., August, 1981.

7. **Caribbean Review,** Vol. VI, No. 4, Fall, 1983, p. 14.

8. Herbert J. Gans, **The Levittowners** (New York: Columbia University Press, 1967). pp. VII-XVII.

9. Maurice R. Stein, **The Eclipse of Community** (New Jersey: Princeton University Press, 1960), p. 320.

10. Interview with Rasta M., August, 1979.

11. Interview with Mr. H.S., August, 1979.

12. Glen Jacobs, (ed.), **The Participant Observers** (New York: George Braziller, Inc., 1970), p.7.

13. Interview with Mr. M.S., July, 1982.

14. Jack D. Douglas, **Investigative Social Research** (Beverly Hills: Sage Publications, 1976), pp. 85-86.

15. See Robert E. Millette **Social Stratification Among Grenadians In Brooklyn** Ph.D. Dissertation, Department of Sociology (New York: New School for Social Research),1982.

16. W.I. Thomas & Florian Znaniecki, **The Polish Peasant In Europe and America** (New York: Alfred A. Knopf 1927), p. 1833.

## Chapter 1

1. Edward J. Cox, "Fedon's Rebellion 1795-96: Causes and Consequences", **Journal of Negro History,** Vol. 67, 1982, p.17.

2. "Population and Vital Statistics Report," A, Vol. XXXIII, No. 2, 1981.

3. Robert C. Kingsbury, Commercial Geography of Grenada, Office of Naval Research Technical Report No. 3 (Bloomington: Indiana University Press, 1960).

4. Allen Eyre, **A New Geography of the Caribbean** (London: George Phillip & Son Ltd.), 1971, p. 57.

5. **West Indian Census,** Part B. Table 55, (Kingston: Government Printery, 1946), p. 43.

6. See Robert E. Millette, **Social Stratification Among Grenadians In Brooklyn** Ph.D. Dissertation, Department of Sociology (New York: New School for Social Research, 1982), p. 75.

7. Raymond T. Smith, **The Negro Family In British Guiana: Family Structure and Social Status in the Villages** (New York: Humanities Press, 1965), p. 67.

8. Judith Blake, **Family Structure In Jamaica: The Social Context of Reproduction** (New York: The Free Press, 1961), p.139.

9. M.G. Smith, **West Indian Family Structure** (Seattle: University of Washington Press, 1962), p. 258.

10. A.W. Singham, **The Hero and The Crowd In A Colonial Polity** (New Haven, Conn: Yale University Press), p. 1968.

11. Joseph Bensman and Arthur Vidich, **The New American Society** (Chicago: Quadrangle Books, 1971), pp. 161-176.

12. Grenada Legislative Council, Order in Council, 1936.

13. **Grenada Yearbook** (St. George's: Grenada Printery, 1967), p. 17.

14. Grenada Legislative Council, Order in Council, 1951.

15. Montserrat was to have one representative.

16. George I. Brizan, **The Grenada Peasantry and Social Revolution 1930-51** (Kingston, Jamaica: Institute of Social and Economic Research, University of the West Indies 1979), p. 29.

## Chapter 2

1. Guenther Roth and Clans Wittich (eds.),Max Weber,**Economy and Society** (Berkeley: University of California Press, 1978), p. 241.

2. D. Sinclair Dabreo, **The Grenada Revolution** (St. Lucia: M.A.P.S. Publication, 1979), p. 29.

3. Erving Goffman, **Presentation of Self in Everyday Life** (New York: Doubleday & Company, Inc., 1959).

4. Interview with Mrs. F.A., August, 1983.

5. Hans Gerth and C. Wright Mills, **From Max Weber: Essays in Sociology** (New York: Oxford University Press, 1946), p. 249.

7. Robert E. Millette, "Can 'Gairyism' Survive in Grenada?" **Everybody's Magazine,** April/May, 1979. p. 34.

8. Arnaldo Hutchinson, "The Long Road to Freedom," **Gramma Weekly Review,** July 12, 1981.

9. **Carib News,** November 1, 1983.

10. Biographical Notes on Maurice Bishop, Grenada: People's Revolutionary Government Pub., n.d. , p. 1.

11. Maurice Bishop, "Forward Ever." Speech given by Maurice Bishop at a Mass rally in St. Georges on the first anniversary of the Grenada Revolution, March 13, 1980. See also, Maurice Bishop, **Forward Ever: Three Years of the Grenada Revolution** (Sydney, Australia: Pathfinder Press, 1982).

12. See Henry Gill, **"The Grenada Revolution: Domestic and Foreign Policy Orientations."** Paper presented at the Caribbean

Studies Association Seventh Annual Conference, Kingston, Jamaica, May 25-29, 1982.

13. Robert Millette, **Social Stratification Among Grenadians in Brooklyn** Ph.D. Dissertation, Department of Sociology (New York: New School for Social Research, 1982) pp 70-71.

14. Chris Searle, **Grenada: The Struggle Against Destibilization** (London: Writers and Readers Publishers, 1983), p. 22.

15. "Report of the Duffus Commission of Inquiry Into The Breakdown of Law and Order, and Police Brutality In Grenada." Jamaica, February 27, 1975. pp. 230-234.

16. A.W. Singham, **The Hero and the Crowd in a Colonial Polity** (New Haven, Conn.: Yale University Press), p. 1968.

17. **Maurice Bishop Speaks: The Grenada Revolution 1979-83** (New York: Pathfinder Press, 1983), p.9.

18. **Black Scholar,** Vol. II, No. 30, Jan.-Feb., 1980, p. 52.

19. A.W. Singham, **The Hero and the Crowd in a Colonial Polity** (New Haven, Conn.: Yale University Press, 1968) p. 152.

20. Chris Searle, **Grenada: The Struggle Against Destabilization** (London: Writers and Readers Publishers 1983) p. 25.

21. Interview with Mr. S.S. November, 1983.

22. Sam Manuel and Andrew Pulley, **Grenada: Revolution in the Caribbean** (New York: Pathfinder Press, 1981), p.6.

23. Interview with Mrs. C.C. January, 1974.

24. Max Weber, (ed.), **The Theory of Social and Economic Organization** (New York: The Free Press, 1947), p. 358.

25. Jack D. Douglas, (ed.), **Deviance and Respectability** (New York: Basic Books, Inc., 1979), p.4.

26. Peter L. Berger and Thomas Luckmann, **The Social Construction of Reality** (Garden City, New York: Doubleday, 1966).

27. Richard Jacobs **The Grenada Revolution At Work** (New York: Pathfinder Press, 1981), p.9.

## Chapter 3

1. D. Sinclair Dabreo, **The Grenada Revolution** (St. Lucia: M.A.P.S. Publication, 1979), p. 117.

2. **Maurice Bishop Speaks: The Grenada Revolution 1979-1983** (New York: Pathfinder Press, 1983) p.14.

3. (p.93)

4. "Grenada: A Preliminary Report." Released by the Department of State and the Department of Defense, Washington, D.C., December 16, 1983. pp. 18-30.

5. Anthony P. Maingot, "Options for Grenada", **Caribbean Review.** p.27.

6. Interview with Mr. A.A. August, 1981.

7. **Trinidad Guardian,** October 15, 1983.

8. **New York Times,** October 17, 1983.

9. **New York Times,** October 18, 1983. See also, **Jamaica Gleaner,** October 24, 1983, and the **Trinidad Guardian,** October 15, 1983.

10. **Trinidad Guardian,** October 16, 1983.

11. **Trinidad Express,** October 18, 1983.

12. **Carib News,** November 1, 1983. See also **Trinidad Guardian,** October 16, 1983.

14. **Trinidad Guardian,** October 19, 1983.

15. **Trinidad Express,** October 17, 1983.

16. **Trinidad Guardian,** October 20, 1983.

17. **New York Times,** October 21, 1983.

18. **Jamaica Gleaner,** October 24, 1983.

19. **Amsterdam Star,** October 20, 1983.

20. **New York News,** October 20, 1983.

21. **Trinidad Express,** October 20, 1983.

22. **Carib News,** October 25, 1983.

23. **Trinidad Guardian,** November 6, 1983.

24. Statement by the Permanent Representative of Trinidad and Tobago in the Security Council on the Question of Grenada. October 28, 1983. pp. 5 and 8. See also, Trinidad Guardian, October 21, 1983.

25. Statement by the Honorable Prime Minister to the House of Representatives of the Parliament of Trinidad and Tobago on October 26, 1983 on the Grenada Crisis, p.3. See also, **Trinidad Guardian,** October 21, 1983.

26. Statement by the Honorable Prime Minister of the House of Representatives of the Parliament of Trinidad and Tobago on October 26, 1983 on the Grenada Crisis, p.3.

27. **Trinidad Guardian,** October 21, 1983.

28. **Trinidad Express,** October 21, 1983.

29. **info '83,** Ministry of Information, Trinidad and Tobago, Volume 9-10 September-October, 1983, p.8.

30. **New York Times,** October 26, 1983.

31. **New York Times,** October 23, 1983.

32. **New York Times,** October 25, 1983.

33. **Amsterdam News,** October 20, 1979. See also **Amsterdam News,** December 19, 1979; **Militant,** August 1, 1980; and **New York Times Magazine,** May 25, 1980.

34. **New York Times Magazine,** May 25, 1980.

35. **New York Daily News,** April 24  1983.

36. **Time Magazine,** May 2, 1983.

37. News Release, Government Information Service, Grenada, July 8, 1981. See also, News Release, Government Information Service, Grenada, June 22, 1981.

38. **Struggle Newspaper,** July 3, 1981.

39. News Release, Government Information Service, Grenada, June 22, 1981.

40. **Trinidad Guardian,** October 27, 1983, p. 116. See also **New**

York Times, October 26, 1983.

41. New York Times, October 27, 1983.

42. Trinidad Guardian, October 27, 1983.

43. New York Times, October 29, 1983.

44. Barbados Advocate, October 30, 1983.

45. Barbados Advocate, October 31, 1983.

46. Trinidad Express, October 14, 1983.

47. New York Times, October 30, 1983.

48. New York Times, October 26, 1983. See also, "The Situation in Grenada." Letter dated November 2, 1983 from the Permanent Representative of Cuba to the United Nations addressed to the Security Council United Nations General Assembly Thirty-eight Session, Agenda Item 145, A-38-554, S-16115 November 3, 1983.

49. New York Times, October 26, 1983. See also, "The Situation in Grenada." Nicaragua and Zimbabwe Draft Resolution. United Nations General Assembly Thirty-eight Session, Agenda Item 145, A-38-L-8., November 1, 1983. pp.1-2.

50. "The Situation in Grenada." Provisional Verbatim Record of the Forty Third Meeting. Held at headquarters, New York, on Wednesday, November 2, 1983 at 3:00 p.m. United Nations General Assembly Thirty-eight Session. Provisional A-38 PV-43, November 5, 1983. For more information on the various issues and who voted and how, see especially pages 13-15, 26, 31, 38-40, 41, 42, 43, 44, 45-50.

51. New York Times, October 28, 1983.

52. New York Times, October 31, 1983.

53. New York Times, November 1, 1983.

54. New York Times, November 3, 1983.

55. New York Times, November 10, 1983.

56. Barbados Advocate, November 4, 1983.

57. New York Times, November 24, 1983.

58. **Barbados Advocate,** November 24, 1983.

59. **Barbados Advocate,** December 24, 1983.

60. **Barbados Advocate,** December 7, 1983.

61. **Barbados Advocate,** November 22, 1983.

**Chapter 4**

1. Mahin Gosine, **Ethnic Heterogeneity and the Black Power Movement in Trinidad: An Historical and Socio-Structural Analysis** (Ann Arbor: University Microfilms, 1982). p. 256.

2. Stokely Carmichael and Charles Hamilton, **Black Power: The Politics of Liberation in America** (New York: Randon House, 1967). See also, Mahin Gosine **Ethnic Heterogeneity and the Black Power Movement** p. 258.

3. Mahin Gosine, **Ethnic Heterogeneity and the Black Power Movement** p. 259. See also, David Nichols, "East Indians and Black Power in Trinidad," **Race,** Vol. 12, No. 4, 1971, pp. 443-459.

4. Maurice Bishop, "The U.S. has Embarked on a Massive Offensive." Opening address at the Socialist International Meeting in Grenada, July 23, 1981.

5. See Maurice Bishop, "Three Years of the Grenada Revolution," **Free West Indian,** March 20, 1982.

6. Maurice Bishop, "Imperialism is the Real Problem." Address to the Organization of American States Conference on the Development Problems of Small Island States in St. Georges on July 13, 1981.

7. **Maurice Bishop Speaks: The Grenada Revolution 1979-83** (New York: Pathfinder Press, 1983), p. XIV.

8. See Merle Hodge and Chris Searle, **Is Freedom We Making: The New Democracy in Grenada** (St. Georges, Grenada: Government Information Service, pub. 1981).

9. Release from the Ministry of Information of the People's Revolutionary Government of Grenada," January, 1980.

10. People's Revolutionary Government, "Benefits to Women Brought by the Grenada Revolution." January, 1980. p.1.

11. See **Grenada is not Alone!** Speeches by the People's Revolutionary Government at the First International Conference in Solidarity with Grenada. (St. Georges, Grenada: Fedon Publishers, 1982) pp. 28-47.

12. See Maurice Bishop, "Women Step Forward" in **Maurice Bishop Selected Speeches** 1971-1981. (Havana: Casa de las Americas, 1982).

13. **New York Times,** August 7, 1983.

14. **Struggle Newspaper,** July 3, 1981.

15. **The Vincentian,** March 31, 1983.

16. **Amsterdam News,** December 19, 1979.

17. **Amsterdam News,** December 4, 1982.

18. **New York Times,** November 22, 1983.

19. **The Vincentian,** March 31, 1983; See also "P.R.G. Statement on U.S. Denial," Government Information Service, Grenada, April 17, 1980.

20. "P.R.G. Statement on U.S. Denial," Government Information Service, Grenada, April 17, 1980.

21. **Amsterdam News,** November 20, 1980.

22. **Trinidad Express,** September 8, 1982.

23. **Amsterdam News,** October 20, 1979.

24. **Amsterdam News,** December 19, 1979.

25. **New York Times Magazine,** May 25, 1980.

26. Statement from the Secretary for National Security on the Illegal Publication of the Grenadian Voice. Government Information Service, Grenada, June 22, 1981. p.1.

27. "No Newspaper until Media Policy is Worked out-PM," Government Information Service, Grenada, June 22, 1981, p. 1.

28. Maurice Jackson, "Grenada's Revolution: The First Two

Years." **Political Affairs,** Vol. 6, June 1981, p. 37.

29. Chris Searle, **Grenada: The Struggle Against Destabilization** (London: Writers and Readers Publishers, 1983). p.59.

30. "The N.Y.O. is for all Patriotic Youths." Grenada: Pamphlet, n.d., p.1.

31. **Trinidad Express,** June 20, 1982.

32. "News Release: Stanley Cyrus and James Herry," Government Information Service, Grenada, July 8, 1981, p.1.

33. **Trinidad Guardian,** October 17, 1983,

34. **Caribbean Review,** Vol. XII, No. 4, 1983, p.12.

35. **Barbados Advocate,** November 19, 1943.

36. See Aaron Segal, "Background to Grenada," **Caribbean Review,** Vol. XXII, No. 4, 1983.

37. **Barbados Advocate,** November 19, 1983. See also, **Amsterdam News,** December 17, 1983.

## Chapter Five

1. Mahin Gosine, **Ethnic Heterogeniety and the Black Movement in Trinidad:** An Historical and Socio-Structrual Analysis, (Ann Arbor: University Microfilms, 1982). p. 301.

2. Robert E. Millette, **Social Stratification Among Grenadians in Brooklyn** Ph.D. Dissertation, Department of Sociology (New York: New School for Social Research, 1982) p. 71.

3. Richard Jacobs and Ian Jacobs, **Grenada: The Route to Revolution** (Havana: Casa de Las Americas, 1979), p.11-21.

4. Henry Gill, **The Grenada Revolution: Domestic and Foreign Policy Orientations,** Paper presented at the Caribbean Studies Association Seventh Annual Conference, Kingston, Jamaica, May 25-29, 1982.

5. **The Vincentian,** March 31, 1983.

6. See "Grenada: A Preliminary Report." pp. 18-30.

7. **Time Magazine,** May 2, 1983, pp. 38-39.

8. See George Beckford,**Persistent Poverty: Underdevelopment in Plantation Economics of the Third World** (New York: Oxford University Press, 1972) p.234.

9. See Raymond T. Smith, "Social Stratification in the Caribbean" in Leonard Plotnikov (eds.), **Essays in Comparative Social Stratification** (Pittsburgh: University of Pittsburgh Press, 1970) pp. 43-76. See also, M.G. Smith, **The Plural Society in the British West Indies** (Berkeley, California: University of California Press, 1965) pp. 262-303.

10. **New York Times,** November 15, 1983.

## Chapter Six

1. Interview with Ms. J.H., July, 1981.

2. See Robert E. Millette, **Social Stratification Among Grenadians in Brooklyn** Ph.D. Dissertation, Department of Sociology (New York: New School for Social Research, 1982).

3. Chris Searle, **Grenada: The Struggle Against Destabilization** (London: Writers and Readers Publishers, 1983) p. 25.

4. Interview with a member of the Central Committee, 1983

5. Interview with Mr. M., June 19, 1984.

6. Interview with a Caribbean Head of State, June, 1984.

7. **Grenadian Voice,** February 25, 1984, p.10.

# BIBLIOGRAPHY

## Books and Articles

Beckford, George. Persistent Poverty: Underdevelopment in Planatation Economies of the Third World. New York: Oxford University Press, 1972.

Bensman, Joseph and Arthur Vidich. The New American Society. Chicago: Quadrangle Books, 1971.

Berger, Peter and Thomas Luckmann. The Social Construction of Reality. Garden City, New York: Doubleday, 1966.

Bilton, Tony et. al. Introductory Sociology. London: Macmillian Press Ltd., 1981.

Biographical Notes on Maurice Bishop. Grenada: People's Revolutionary Government Pub., n.d.

Black Scholar. Vol. II, No. 3, Jan. - Feb. 1980.

Blake, Judith. Family Structure in Jamaica: The Social Context of Reproduction. New York: Free Press, 1961.

Bishop, Maurice. "Forward Ever". Speech given by Maurice Bishop at a mass rally in St. George's on the first anniversary of the Grenada Revolution, March 13, 1980.

Bishop, Maurice. "Cuba, Nicaragua, Grenada: Together We Shall Win". Speech delivered in Revolution Square, Havana, Cuba, May 1, 1980.

# BIBLIOGRAPHY

Bishop, Maurice. "Imperialism is the Real Problem". Address to the Organization of American States Conference on the Development Problems of Small Island States in St. George's, July 13, 1981.

Bishop, Maurice. "The U.S. has Embarked on a Massive Offensive". Opening address at the Socialist International Meeting in Grenada, July 23, 1981.

Bishop, Maurice. "Women Step Forward" in Maurice Bishop Selected Speeches 1979-1981. Havana: Casa de las Americas, 1982.

Bishop, Maurice. "Three Years of the Grenada Revolution". Free West Indian, March 20, 1982.

Bishop, Maurice. Forward Ever: Three Years of the Grenada Revolution. Sydney, Australia: Pathfinder Press, 1982.

Braithwaite, Lloyd. "Social Stratification in Trinidad". Social and Economic Studies, Vol. 2, October 1953, pp. 5-173.

Brizan, George I. The Grenada Peasantry and Social Revolution, 1930-1951. Kingston, Jamaica: Institute of Social and Economic Research, University of the West Indies, 1979.

Caribbean Review. Vol. XII, No. 4, Fall, 1983.

Carmichael, Stokeley and Charles Hamilton. Black Power: The Politics of Liberation in America. New York: Random House, 1967.

Cox, Edward L. "Fedon's Rebellion 1795-96: Causes and Consequences". Journal of Negro History, Vol. 67, 1982.

Dabreo, D. Sinclair. The Grenada Revolution. St. Lucia: Management Advertising and Publicity Services Pub., 1979.

Douglas, Jack D. Investigative Social Research. Beverly Hills, Cal.: Sage Pub., 1976.

Emmanuel, Patrick. Crown Colony Politics in Grenada, 1917-1951. Cave Hill, Barbados: Institute of Social and Economic Research, University of the West Indies, 1978.

Eyre, Allen. A New Geography of the Caribbean. London: George Phillip and Son, Ltd., 1971.

Freire, Paulo. Pedagogy of the Oppressed. New York: Herder and Herder Pub., 1970.

Gans, Herbert J. The Levittowners. New York: Columbia University Press, 1967.

Gerth, Hans and C. Wright Mills. From Max Weber: Essays in Sociology. New York: Oxford University Press, 1946.

Goffman, Erving. Presentation of Self in Everyday Life. New York: Doubleday and Co., Inc., 1959.

Gosine, Mahin. Ethnic Heterogeneity and the Black Power Movement in Trinidad: An Historical and Socio-Structural Analysis. Ann Arbor: University Microfilms, 1982.

Grenada Legislative Council, Order in Council, 1936.

Grenada Legislative Council, Order in Council, 1951.

Grenada Yearbook, 1967.

Grenada is not Alone. Speeches by the People's Revolutionary Government at the First International Conference in Solidarity with Grenada. St. George's, Grenada: Fedon Publishers, 1982.

"Grenada: A Preliminary Report". Released by the Department of State and the Department of Defense, Washington, D.C., December 16, 1983.

Henry, Gill. "The Grenada Revolution: Domestic and Foreign Policy Orientations". Paper presented at the Caribbean Studies Association Seventh Annual Conference, Kingston, Jamaica, May 25-29, 1982.

Hodge, Merle and Chris Searle. Is Freedom We Making: The New Democracy in Grenada. St. George's, Grenada: Government Information Service Pub., 1981.

# BIBLIOGRAPHY

Hutchinson, Arnaldo. "The Long Road to Freedom". Gramma Weekly Review, July 12, 1981.

Info-83, Ministry of Information, Trinidad and Tobago, Vol. 9-10, September-October, 1983.

Jackson, Maurice. "Grenada's Revolution: The First Two Years". Political Affairs, Vol. 6, June 1981.

Jacobs, Glen. (ed.), The Participant Observers. New York: George Braziller, Inc., 1970.

Jacobs, Richard and Ian Jacobs. Grenada: The Route to Revolution. Havana: Casa de las Americas, 1979.

Jacobs, Richard. The Grenada Revolution at Work. New York: Pathfinder Press. 1981.

Kingsbury, Robert C. Commercial Geography of Grenada. Office of Naval Research Technical Report No. 3. Bloomington: Indiana University Press, 1960. .

Knight, E. Giddens. The Grenada Handbook and Directory.

Machiavelli, Niccolo. The Prince. New York: The New American Library, 1952.

Maingot, Anthony. "Options for Grenada". Caribbean Review, Vol. XII, No. 4, Fall, 1983.

Manuel, Sam and Andrew Pulley. Grenada: Revolution in the Caribbean. New York: Pathfinder Press, 1981.

Millette, Robert. "Can Gairyism Survive in Grenada?" Everybody's Magazine, April-May, 1979.

Millette, Robert. Social Stratification Among Grenadians in Brooklyn. Ph.D. Dissertation. Department of Sociology. New York: New School for Social Research, 1982.

News Release. Government Information Service, Grenada, June 22,

1981.

"No Newspapers until Media Policy is Worked Out - P.M." Government Information Service, Grenada, June 22, 1981.

New Release. Government Information Service, Grenada, July 8, 1981.

News Release: Stanley Cyrus and James Herry, Government Information Service, Grenada, July 8, 1981.

Nichols, David. "East Indians and Black Power in Trinidad". Race, Vol. 12, No. 4, pp. 443-459.

People's Revolutionary Government. "Benefits to Women Brought by the Grenada Revolution", January, 1980.

People's Revolutionary Government Statement on U.S. Denial. Government Information Service, Grenada, April 17, 1980.

Population and Vital Statistics Report. New York: United Nations, Series A, Vol. XXXIII, No. 2, 1981.

Release from the Ministry of Information of the People's Revolutionary Government of Grenada. January, 1980.

Report of the Duffus Commission of Inquiry into the Breakdown of Law and Order, and Police Brutality in Grenada. Jamaica: February 27, 1975.

Roth, Guenther and Clans Wittich. (eds.), Max Weber, Economy and Society. Berkeley: University of California Press, 1978.

Scott, Marvin B. and Stanford M. Lyman. The Revolt of the Students. Ohio: Charles E. Merrill Pub. Co., 1970.

Searle, Chris. Grenada: The Struggle Against Destabilization. London: Writers and Readers Pub., 1983.

Segal, Aaron, "Background to Grenada". Caribbean Review, Vol. XII, No. 4, 1983.

# BIBLIOGRAPHY

Singham, Archibald. The Hero and the Crowd in a Colonial Polity. New Haven, Conn.: Yale University Press, 1968.

Singham, Archibald. The Colonial Political System: A Case Study of Political Conflict in a British Colony. Ann Arbor: University Microfilms, 1969.

Smith, M.G. West Indian Family Structure. Seattle: University of Washington Press, 1962.

Smith, M.G. The Plural Society in the British West Indies. Berkeley: University of California Press, 1965.

Smith, Raymond T. The Negro Family in British Guiana: Family Structure and Social Status in the Village. New York: Humanities Press, 1961.

Smith, Raymond T. "Social Stratification in the Caribbean" in Leonard Plotnikov (ed.), Essays in Comparative Social Stratification. Pittsburgh: University of Pittsburgh, 1970.

"Statement from the Secretary for National Security on the Illegal Publication of the Grenadian Voice". Government Information Service, Grenada, June 22, 1981.

"Statement by the Honorable Prime Minister to the House of Representatives of the Parliament of Trinidad and Tobago on October 26, 1983 on the Grenada Crisis". Consulate General of the Republic of Trinidad and Tobago.

"Statement by the Permanent Representative of Trinidad and Tobago in the Security Council on the Question of Grenada". October 28, 1983.

Stein, Maurice R. The Eclipse of Community. New Jersey: Princeton University Press, 1960.

"The Situation in Grenada". Nicaragua and Zimbabwe Draft Resolution, United Nations General Assembly Thirty-eight Session, Agenda Item 145, A - 38 - L8, November 1, 1983.

"The Situation in Grenada". Letter dated 2 November 1983 from the Permanent Representative of Cuba to the United Nations addressed to the Security Council. United Nations General Assembly Thirty-eight Session, Agenda Item 145, A-38-554, S-16115, November 3, 1983.

"The Situation in Grenada". Provisional Verbatim record of the Forty-Third Meeting. Held at headquarters, New York, on Wednesday, 2 November 1983 at 3 p.m. United Nations General Assembly Thirty-eight Session, Provisional A-38, P.V. 43, November 5, 1983.

"The N.Y.O. is for all Patriotic Youth". Grenada, Pamphlet, n.d.

Thomas, W.I. and Florian Znaniecki. The Polish Peasant in Europe and America. New York: Alfred A. Knopf Pub., 1927.

Weber, Max (ed.), The Theory of Social and Economic Organization. New York: Free Press, 1947.

West Indian Census. Part B, Table 55. Kingston: Government Printery, 1946.

### Newspapers

Amsterdam News, October 20, 1979.
Amsterdam News, December 19, 1979.
Amsterdam News, November 20, 1980.
Amsterdam News, December 4, 1982.
Amsterdam News, October 20, 1983.
Amsterdam News, October 22, 1983.
Amsterdam News, December 17, 1983.
Barbados Advocate, October 30, 1983.
Barbados Advocate, October 31, 1983.
Barbados Advocate, November 4, 1983.
Barbados Advocate, November 19, 1983.
Barbados Advocate, November 22, 1983.
Barbados Advocate, November 24, 1983.
Barbados Advocate, December 7, 1983.
Barbados Advocate, December 18, 1983.
Barbados Advocate, December 21, 1983.

# BIBLIOGRAPHY

Barbados Advocate, December 24, 1983.
Carib News, October 25, 1983.
Carib News, November 1, 1983.
Jamaica Gleaner, October 24, 1983.
Militant, August 1, 1980.
New York Daily News, April 24, 1983.
New York Times, October 17, 1983.
New York Times, October 18, 1983.
New York Times, October 21, 1983.
New York Times, October 23, 1983.
New York Times, October 25, 1983.
New York Times, October 26, 1983.
New York Times, October 27, 1983.
New York Times, October 28, 1983.
New York Times, October 29, 1983.
New York Times, October 30, 1983.
New York Times, October 31, 1983.
New York Times, November 1, 1983.
New York Times, November 3, 1983.
New York Times, November 10, 1983.
New York Times, November 15, 1983.
New York Times, November 22, 1983.
New York Times, February 8, 1984.
New York Times, February 9, 1984.
Struggle, July 3, 1981.
Trinidad Express, June 20, 1982.
Trinidad Express, September 8, 1982.
Trinidad Express, October 14, 1983.
Trinidad Express, October 15, 1983.
Trinidad Express, October 16, 1983.
Trinidad Express, October 17, 1983.
Trinidad Express, October 18, 1983.
Trinidad Express, October 20, 1983.
Trinidad Express, October 21, 1983.
Trinidad Guardian, October 16, 1983.
Trinidad Guardian, October 17, 1983.
Trinidad Guardian, October 19, 1983.
Trinidad Guardian, October 20, 1983.
Trinidad Guardian, October 21, 1983.
Trinidad Guardian, October 27, 1983.
Trinidad Guardian, November 6, 1983.

Vincentian, March 31, 1983.

## Magazines

New York Times Magazine, May 25, 1980.
New York Times Magazine, August 7, 1983.
Time Magazine, May 2, 1983.
Time Magazine, October 31, 1983.
Time Magazine, November 7, 1983.
Time Magazine, November 14, 1983.
Time Magazine, November 21, 1983.

## Interviews

Interview with Mrs. F.A. 1963.
Interview with Mrs. C.S. January, 1974.
Interview with Mr. B.B. August, 1979.
Interview with Rasta M. August, 1979.
Interview with Mr. H.S. Summer, 1981.
Interview with Mr. M.S. July, 1982.
Interview with Mr. S.S. November, 1983.

# NAME INDEX

# SUBJECT INDEX